Bodacious
The Shepherd Cat

Bodacious

The Shepherd Cat

A Charming Tale of an
Extraordinary
Cat

SUZANNA CRAMPTON

HARPER
element

HarperElement
An imprint of HarperCollins*Publishers*
1 London Bridge Street
London SE1 9GF

www.harpercollins.co.uk

First published by HarperCollins*Publishers* 2018

1 3 5 7 9 10 8 6 4 2

A catalogue record of this book is
available from the British Library

ISBN 978-0-00-829575-2

Printed and bound in Australia by
McPherson's Printing Group

MIX
Paper from
responsible sources
FSC
www.fsc.org
FSC C007454

This book is produced from independently certified FSC paper
to ensure responsible forest management

For more information visit: www.harpercollins.co.uk/green

To my parents, Julia and Richard Crampton

'We abuse land because we see it as a commodity belonging to us. When we see land as a community to which we belong, we may begin to use it with love and respect.'

ALDO LEOPOLD

Contents

PART III: AUTUMN

PART IV: WINTER

Introduction

I am Bodacious, The Shepherd Cat, and this is my story. I wasn't always called Bodacious. I must have been called something else in my kittenhood in the nearby city of Kilkenny, but it's all a bit of a mystery to my human. As far as she's concerned, I appeared one day and have never left. It's a secret I plan to keep.

The Shepherd told me the story of how she found me so many times and added so many embellishments that it's almost become a fairy 'tail'. She walked into a Kilkenny flower shop one day in search of red ribbon for a friend's birthday present, a clear-glass handblown goblet with herbs planted in it. She described it in great detail: about the herbs being green, the soil brown, and the ribbon a deep red. (The Shepherd gets very excited about this kind of thing.) The florist goes by the romantic name of Lamber de Bie and the shop is tucked away on a narrow cobbled street near Kilkenny Castle. The lady who worked there, Jaszia, told The Shepherd that because it was just after Valentine's Day, she was out of red ribbon but she did have a cat.

'Maybe you might be interested in him,' Jaszia said, knowing The Shepherd only too well. 'You know the shop that sells the novelty toilet seats just down the hill towards the castle? Well, there's a cat there that walked in off the streets. Sadly, the shop owner can't keep him as she has three dogs at home.'

'I'll go down and have a look,' said The Shepherd. Of course she said she'd have a look – she loves animals and has a whole menagerie of us on the family farm, but more of that later. She told me that when she came into the shop, she saw me wandering around in amidst all of these brightly coloured transparent plastic toilet seats. They were all full of strange things like barbed wire, straw, even coral reefs and tropical fish. She, of course, assumed I owned the place, but I had only been there for three days. Cheeky! As if a place that sold novelty toilet seats would in any way be suitable for a cat like me. She also told me that I was found wearing a pink collar with pictures of blue mice running around it – clearly somebody's idea of a joke, but it showed that once, someone else loved me, too.

The shop owner had done everything possible to find my original owner, and there wasn't a person in Kilkenny who hadn't heard the radio appeal, but no one came forward. I could be sad about that, I suppose, but I'm not, because if I hadn't walked into the toilet-seat shop a few days before, I would never have met The Shepherd. I would never have had the life I have now on Black Sheep Farm, in small green fields above the banks of the River Nore. The land has been in The Shepherd's family for many generations, so every building and field has a name and a known unwritten history, like the Wind-Charger Field, where once a windmill stood and spun to generate electricity for the farm in the 1940s.

The Shepherd kept me inside at first, because she said she didn't want me to disappear again, at least not until I knew the place as home. It was thoughtful of her, but what she didn't know was that I thought of it as home from the moment I set foot in it. Still, for two weeks I curled up by the Aga, or looked out the window at the huge horse chestnut trees with mountains beyond, which were quite pleasant. I got to know others in my family, too, which was useful because I was able to establish myself firmly as almost Top Cat.

I was trained in the ways of farm life by Oscar, now long gone. He was an odd-looking feline, with his pure white body possessing a few sizeable tabby spots, tabby ears and a tabby tail that looked as if it had been painted and stuck on as an afterthought. Later, there came Miss Marley, whose owners had emigrated to New Zealand and couldn't afford the expensive quarantine. She is a shy, unassuming feminine feline, who loves her job as wool inspector. I allow her this important task, even though all she ever does is test its softness by curling up and falling asleep on piles of raw wool, or sometimes even on our woven blankets made of wool from our rare-breed Zwartbles sheep, just before they are shipped off to some distant place in the world.

Cat Ovenmitt, my Shepherd Cat apprentice, was another late arrival, which is just as well, because, frankly, he has a lot to learn – and he is bog lazy. He acquired his name soon after he was brought to the farm. The Shepherd's mother had opened the Aga door and she reached over for what she thought was an oven mitt to pull out a roast chicken. When her hand landed on the then nameless new member of the menagerie, she remarked, 'Oh, I thought you were an oven mitt.' And so he was baptised. His aims in life are to spend as much time as possible with his grey-black tabby body stretched out against our kitchen's warm Aga or in a big bowl on top of our tall kitchen press, cosy from rising Aga heat. One of his favourite sports is to annoy Miss Marley as often as possible. His most recent favourite toy, much to my disgust, is the new canine Puddlemaker (more about her later), who is hardly bigger than a rat.

*

I also met my best canine friend at Black Sheep Farm: a slightly scruffy Border Collie/Fox Terrier cross named Pepper, a handsome fellow, with his black wiry coat and lightly salted beard. Over the years I've watched his coat mature into a distinguished-looking full-bodied mix of salt and pepper colours. 'The Einstein of dogs' is what many humans call him, joking that if he were human, he'd probably be a bearded pipe-smoking scholarly writer. He is, most importantly, a tenacious ratter and hunter of grey squirrels and rabbits, of which there are plenty on the farm. The softer-hearted among you might see this as terrible cruelty, but I have learned so much about nature since I began to lead my agrarian life here. Rodents would destroy everything if we let their population boom. They eat and foul hay and grains and even chew electric wires, which could cause fires. Rabbits, if they overpopulate, catch a terrible virus called myxomatosis, which means that their population plummets and foxes and buzzards go hungry. Grey squirrels kill our native red squirrel and also strip bark off young trees, which kills them or stunts their growth. The Shepherd is passionate about her trees and gets very upset when she finds one squirrel-stripped.

The Shepherd adopted Pepper from a local puppy rescue centre. Someone had brought him there after he had been discovered with his siblings in a paper bag on the side of a busy road, not far from Black Sheep Farm. The kindly woman who runs the puppy rescue did not want money or even a contribution of dog food to the centre in return for the adoption. Instead, she asked for a small basket of figs. She remembered that many years before, she had visited the farm and The Shepherd's grandfather had given her a delicious freshly plucked ripe fig to eat. (Long ago, The Shepherd's great-great-grandmother had planted half a dozen fig trees that had flourished against the stone walls in the garden and those trees still produced scrumptious figs every summer.) The Shepherd explained that figs wouldn't be ready to pick for some months as they didn't ripen till some time in August. The kindly lady said that was fine. She could, and would, wait as she recalled that her fig had been so memorably delicious.

Months later, The Shepherd brought her a small basket full of fresh ripe figs as the purchase price for Pepper. She also brought him along to show how well he had matured into a lovely dog. But when the car door opened at the canine rescue centre Pepper told me that he took one whiff of the local air and refused point-blank to exit the car. The poor fellow thought The Shepherd was about to return him. He sat trembling on the car floor, terrified of what might unfold. The Shepherd comforted him and left him in the car while she delivered the basket of figs. The lady was delighted, Pepper later told me, because, as it happened, she had completely forgotten the planned exchange.

The matriarch canine when I arrived here on Black Sheep Farm was Tassie. She had also been adopted by The

Shepherd from the kindly lady at the rescue centre. She was a pure-white coarse-haired, tenacious Jack Russell Terrier, who was terrified of nearly everything because of her experience at a previously abusive home, but her main passion in life, when not cleaved to The Shepherd like a shadow, was hunting rats. She was brilliant at her job, even climbing trees and walls in pursuit of her prey. People would often phone The Shepherd to bring Tassie to their house when they had cornered a rat, as she was so very quick and efficient at dispatching them.

It is my understanding that The Big Fellow arrived as a small black puppy who could fit into a shopping bag. He is a large black wolf-like German Shepherd. When I first arrived and heard his bark, I would nearly jump out of my furry skin. It was truly deafening, but I now know that his bark disguises a heart like a soft marshmallow.

Then there is capricious Bear, who arrived here more recently as a tiny pup, so used to be known as the Puddle-maker. Puddlemaker is an apt name for young canines as all they seem capable of is leaving puddles all across the kitchen floor, which we must all navigate around until they're cleaned up. A mixed mutt, Bear has the nose-scenting prowess of a Beagle, the glossy fluffy coat of a King Charles Spaniel, the tenacity of a Jack Russell Terrier and the disloyalty of a Labrador. His stubby turned-out legs make him look like a very odd Corgi. His mother had been a rescued canine whose new owners had mistakenly allowed her to get pregnant. She had been at the vet's to get the procedure when she was discovered to be in pup.

Bear, I merely tolerate, but as for the new Puddlemaker, well … she is small with a black-brown coat, with ears that are far too large for her tiny body, which give the impression of a fruit bat, and a pert upright tail that some humans call 'cute'. To me, she is a nuisance, even with her sophisticated Peruvian name – Inca!!! The time can't come soon enough when she learns how to respect and behave towards authority. Meanwhile, I am quite happy to oblige in her further education with well-aimed clawed smacks at appropriate moments convenient to myself.

The Shepherd loves the canine's fruit-bat face as it reminds her of her time in Borneo many years ago, when she worked for a wildlife charity. She once took a boat trip out into a tidal mangrove rainforest to look at proboscis monkeys in their natural habitat. They've a funny long flat nose that protrudes from their face and a large pot belly. After a successful trip of quietly manoeuvring around jungled mangrove islands to see these primates the boats headed back towards Brunei city. As sunset approached, the air filled with a chattering noise on whispering wings of thousands upon thousands of flying foxes as they set off to hunt for fruit. These large bats have a fox-like face and pointed ears much like our new Puddlemaker.

When I first arrived at the farm, I didn't even have a name. I was simply called 'Puss-woossh' or 'Pritty Kitty Cat', which is a bit demeaning, particularly as I am so handsome. People often ask what I am, with my big green eyes, pointed ears and coat of fluffy brown-black fur. What a stupid question. I'm a cat, of course – not a Maine Coon or a Norwegian Forest cat, but a Kilkenny cat at that.

Anyway, when The Shepherd finally let me out from the snug warmth of the Aga, I followed her around – she was kind of interesting after all, with her mane of long, grey hair and strong voice, the better to reach the end of fields when she calls our beloved sheep.

At the time of my arrival, she kept horses in stables in a small outer farmyard with low stone sheds and buildings. On this particular morning, she strode across to the stables, where two horses looked out over their half-doors. She buckled on their head collars and opened both stable doors, saying, 'Stand!' in a firm voice to both horses; they stood stone-still and didn't budge, which I found quite impressive. I walked between two of them to get a better look. They were certainly very tall, with their shiny coats, one bay and one grey with silky manes, quite handsome even if they were horses. Horses, as we all know, aren't that intelligent most of the time. (The exception being Marco Polo – more about him later.)

'Silly cat,' The Shepherd said when she noticed me underfoot. She nudged me with her boot to get out of the way as she was about to lead both horses forward, my guess is in case I got trodden on by one of their great hooves as they walked out into the cobbled yard. Their huge muscular bodies towered above me. She thought I was scared, but she was wrong: I don't do 'scared'. I continued to walk alongside her between the two horses, not at all bothered by their size or the metallic sound their shod hooves made as they walked across cobbles towards the field gate.

'Oh, my God!' she exclaimed when I wouldn't budge. 'You are sooooo bodacious, do you know that?' So, Bodacious I became.

She's since bored me often enough with this story of how that word, a Cajun term, comes from the bayous of Louisiana. It seems to mean, 'Big, bold, beautiful, bolshie', which I suppose is accurate enough. Apparently, it reminds her of her younger self as others called her that when she was a spirited young woman living in New York City, a long time ago in cat years. Even though Black Sheep Farm has been part of The Shepherd's family for two hundred years, part of her family comes from America.

That was long ago – nine or ten years – and I decided to stay. There was something about this house, orchard and fields that made me want to take part in life here, not for the usual reasons – a plentiful supply of food and rodents – but because I felt at home here: sunning myself in a corner of the garden that looks down to a faded mellow pink farmhouse, or nosing around in the orchard. Besides, I knew that The Shepherd needed me. She barely managed before I came along, though Pepper had made a great and dedicated effort.

Once I'd made the decision, I had to find a role for myself in The Shepherd's animal family. I shadowed Oscar, the white cat with tabby spots. He looked as if he was in charge, so I simply followed his lead. When there were lambs under a red heat lamp, Oscar would join them. He'd curl up underneath it to add to their collected warmth. There was nothing in it for him, needless to say.

Oscar died in 2013, and I must say, I miss him. There's no one around to share the burden of being Top Shepherd Cat and the responsibilities that go with it. For there are many: I mostly instruct, oversee and keep The Shepherd company during long hours of lambing. I watch over the fields as she tops long grasses in well-grazed meadows. I help bring in hay, check stock during feeding time, assist in early lamb care for those who need help to start their lives.

I am not Little Bo-Peep, though we have lost some sheep on occasion when they've escaped through broken fences or over old fallen stone walls into neighbours' fields. I have learned to expect a rough-with-smooth life and an occasional death. To tend sheep is hard work. My Shepherd believes in sustainable farming, so we must feed soil naturally to grow a healthy variety of grasses, clovers, herbs and wild-meadow flowers. All these plants feed sheep that grow wool that is shorn, cleaned, spun and woven into warm beautiful blankets (designed by The Shepherd) at a local woollen mill, Cushendale, in the lovely village of Graiguenamanagh. These blankets are then sent all over the world: even our President of Ireland has one – but more of that later. There will be plenty of sheep in this book. Some sheep are harvested for meat, others are sold to become breeding stock on another farm.

I'm just a minor shepherd if one compares my flock to the Australian or New Zealand flocks and their many thousands of white woolly sheep. My flock is small: just sixty to eighty in size, most of which are a rare breed of sheep called Zwartbles. They are large chocolate-coloured beasts with a long white blaze on their face, a white tip to the tail and a pair of white bobby socks on their back legs. They are a bit dim, but easy enough to manage. They provide lots of milk that can produce delicious cheese or sumptuously delectable ice cream, which The Shepherd has made and which is whisker-licking good. Their lovely fleeces are a fine rich dark chocolate brown, like espresso coffee.

I also find that I have to look after The Shepherd from time to time. As I mentioned earlier, long ago she worked for a wildlife charity in Southeast Asia. She befriended many exotic wild animals while she collected and collated animal-husbandry and veterinary information to bring home to her employer in London. This was before you could google such specialist information and find correct answers. While there, she contracted a tropical sickness which kept her bedridden for three years. Although this illness lingers, she manages capably with my help and enjoys her farm work, although I still have to play nursemaid to her whenever she succumbs to a recurrence. I lie on her to keep her stationary, so that she rests. It's a hard life.

On top of this, I give instructions while The Shepherd cooks and I make sure all the eggs are collected from my egg-makers. They might think their eggs are hidden, but I know where they hide them, behind bales of straw and nestled in loose hay. I also keep other animals in check and I'm not above giving one of them a clawed slap to keep them under control. When The Shepherd is working in the garden I make sure the robin doesn't get all the worms, leaving some behind to naturally enrich the soil – it's simple really, I just chase him away from the top of the garden fork. I ignore Miss Marley, but I must always control Ovenmitt to show him who is the main Shepherd Cat.

My work never ends, but my day usually debuts when I feel like it. Sometimes it begins when the scullery door to the house opens and I enter to breakfast on crunchy cat biscuits. Other days start by counting sheep with The Shepherd and our canine work companions. I find the most accurate way to check sheep is to count the legs and divide by four.

I enjoy walks through the fields to inspect ewes and lambs. Some are old friends whom I greet with a gentle welcome salutation of a headbutt. Others try to headbutt me, so I tend to avoid them. Ram lambs can be quite stroppy, so I must watch out for them in particular. Mostly all is well as we walk through fields to count ewes and lambs, check fences, stone walls and note what the wildlife is doing as each year turns. All that counting sheep can make me feel a bit sleepy though, so afterwards I sometimes catch a snooze in front of or on top of the Aga.

After more than twenty years in charge, The Shepherd is passably competent and the benefits of supervising her outweigh the disadvantages, so I do not plan to move on at this time. But I am a singularly independent cat and I should never be taken for granted. I am NOT child-friendly and I do not suffer fools gladly. I am a busy professional, intelligent – if I say so myself – hard-working farm cat. Humans have tried to pick me up, but quickly drop me when my teeth sink into their hands or arms. When teased, my claws quickly find exposed flesh. The only human I respect is my own human, The Shepherd. As she is a female farmer, she will sometimes be patronised by male humans and asked to show someone where the 'real boss' is. She can't really point to me and say, 'There's my boss', or they might laugh even harder, even if we both know it to be true.

On cold misty mornings when we walk up and down rolling green hills of the 14 acres of our part of a 50-acre farm,
mist from our exhaled breath fills the air. We feel we are on
our own until all of our flock of sheep troop up to us,
baa-ing, out of the misty banks of air. When a cold winter
sun leaks weak milky light and frost whitens the ground in
dark dawn of day, black shapes linger far across fields and
then draw close as they are called for breakfast. The rattle of
the Magic Bucket of sheep nuts lures them towards us.

Of course, many jobs other than winter-feeding must be
done. I like to oversee the vaccination and dosing for worms
of sheep and lambs in particular. I sit on a wooden work-
table or on a ledge of an old stone wall that overlooks the
working sheep yard. I chat with a sheep occasionally as The
Shepherd vaccinates or doses each one. When farm machinery needs a grease or service I stand by to supervise. I enjoy
gardening and when not directing The Shepherd as she digs,
I sleep in the deep cool shade of box hedges. If someone
passes and I wake up, I always shout, 'Meow' to say, 'Hello'
and rise up out of my cosy bed to steer them towards another
job. Farming is like that: there are always a thousand jobs to
do and many of them never get done. For farmers a weekend
is still a weather dependent daily job dictated by season not
hours or a categorised allotment of days.

In rain, sun, snow and wind I pad down laneways, cross
winter streams, carefully walk through muddy gateways,

weave my way through long summer grasses, jump on to the tops of fence posts to survey my flock of sheep, or wander along tops of walls to view them from a great height. So far my fluffy tail has never been closed in a gate, but I have sometimes been left on the wrong side and have had to crawl under or through it – most undignified. Mind you, I'm quite immune to wet muddy yards now as my city-slicker days of long ago and my distant youth are far behind me. This is my life now and I wouldn't wish it any different.

Part I
SPRING

1
Egg-makers and Spring Flowers

During the mucky, muddy month of March on Black Sheep Farm there is a unique sight to behold as daffodils flower. In what is called the 'middle lawn' field, it looks like the sun has gone splat and landed there. There are at least twenty-one different kinds of daffodil that flower and there could be more. The Shepherd's grandparents planted all the bulbs many years before my time. This is how they earned their livelihood – by selling flowers and vegetables at local markets.

Black Sheep farmhouse, with its lovely pale yellow and pink exterior, now covered with a thick layer of ivy, its fine porch supported by four Tuscan columns (not installed by the Tuscans, obviously, but much later), its large slate roof, and its warm stone outhouses, has been in The Shepherd's family for generations. She occasionally pulls a dusty old book, dated 1801, off the shelf to show guests the history of our farm. I always sneeze when she opens that creaking book with its cracked leather binding. She indicates where her triple great-grandfather wrote long ago about sheep farming. In those distant, now almost foreign times, a horse or donkey powered the plough. Many flocks of sheep had their standards and qualities measured by how many cheeses their milk made per day from the milk collected. Back then, sheep gave birth, kept their lambs only six weeks before weaning and all ewes were milked (today, with modern farming, most flocks of sheep are farmed just for their meat). There are a few dairies these days that milk sheep and more coming on line in Ireland as humans become aware of how delicious sheep's milk is, much to The Shepherd's delight. The farmers produced delicious cheeses from sheep's milk that were then sold weekly in nearby Kilkenny city. In those days, with no refrigeration, sheep's milk lasted longer, never soured and kept its fine flavour better when it was made into cheese. So, sheep that could be milked and whose milk produced a lot of cheeses were considered a superior flock. Cow's milk was a rival, but when made into butter or cheese tainted more easily in pre-refrigeration days. Sheep's cheese was more durable.

Nowadays, as well as using the wool to make fine woollen blankets, The Shepherd still follows many other agrarian tasks that she learned from her grandparents when she was a little girl, visiting Black Sheep Farm from her home, which was then thousands of miles away in America.

Unlike myself, an Irish-born Kilkenny city feline, The Shepherd was born in New York City, where her father (now a tall, still-handsome man with a stoop and a diligent, calm manner) worked in city hospitals. When The Shepherd was born, she was not a completely well child. It was soon discovered she was allergic to cow's milk. In fact, soon after I arrived on the farm, The Shepherd and her mother were cleaning out a tall press in the kitchen when they discovered on the top shelf hidden at the back a big blue-grey tin of Gerber's baby soy milk. It still had the price tag and label from a Belfast shop. The Shepherd wanted to save it as a souvenir but her ma did not, saying, 'When you were a baby, you were so thin, people thought I was starving you.'

The Shepherd is lucky to have known all her grandparents and some elderly cousins to whom she could ask questions about her family history. Her bloodlines are about as pure as our mixed mutt, Bear. Her hodgepodge American-Irish ancestry reflects input from Ireland, Scotland, England, colonial Maryland and Ukraine. Farming runs deep in her blood, though. On her paternal side her many times great grandfather was born in 1735, in Maryland, where he farmed in Pleasant Valley, Washington County, a mile or so west of Crampton's Gap in South Mountain, a north extension of the Blue Ridge Mountains.

The Shepherd's paternal grandfather was a very handsome Don Juan, who pursued many beautiful well-known women between and during his first three marriages. He abandoned his first wife (The Shepherd's grandmother), who was a successful journalist and fashion writer in the 1920s, when The Shepherd's father was very young and his sister just a baby. His mother, Louise, survived the Great Depression as a single parent and supported her children through her careers in Benton & Bowles advertising firm in New York and editing the Connecticut state guide book. When finances were difficult, kind farmers let her glean leftover potatoes and carrots from harvested fields. The Shepherd's father remembers how his mother would create a sense of picnic and adventure as she roasted their meagre dinner in the fireplace of their small farmhouse in rural Connecticut. Now, vegetables and fresh, tasty lamb are plentiful on Black Sheep Farm, but the thrift and care that The Shepherd learned from her parents and grandparents has never left her.

When The Shepherd and I are gone, my beautiful Zwartbles flock will disperse and the farmstead will pass on to its next inhabitant. The Shepherd's only wish is that her philosophy of steady improvement of farmland will continue with whomever comes after her. She fell in love with country life and sundry farming tasks as a child. Her mother's family has farmed this land hereabouts in Ireland for many generations and from her maternal Irish grandfather, whose family had owned Black Sheep Farm, she learned how to look after and harvest vegetables, red- and blackcurrants and raspberries in his market garden. He also taught her how to pick and box apples, pears and plums from his orchard. Her Irish grandmother taught her how to bed and grow flowers and cut and arrange bunches to sell. Her maternal grandfather called himself a market gardener, but he was also a gifted writer of five books of acclaimed essays. Her grandmother was a painter and poet, and she also fostered many children during the Second World War and other troubled times.

In the USA at her Maryland cousins' farm, The Shepherd learned how to milk cows by hand, befriended the sheep and began to understand the rudiments of tending their flock. The cousins also bred championship ponies, which is how she first learned to ride, and only bareback at that. She later learned how to gentle the wild young ponies to the human touch. She often surprised people when she took a saddle off a horse before riding it, saying that she was uncomfortable in a saddle because she couldn't feel a horse's intention with the saddle between them. Now, as a much older woman, she enjoys the luxury of riding in a saddle.

Here on Black Sheep Farm, when orphaned lambs are brought outside from their shed – where they're normally housed, warmed by heat lamps – for daily walks of fresh air and grass-shoot nibbles, The Shepherd is like a pied piper.

Weaving her way through our field of yellow and white daffodils with a menagerie of lambs, the canine crew and my apprentice Ovenmitt cavort behind her. Lambs race about among the flowers while Ovenmitt plays a bouncing game of hide and seek. He will pounce out, prancing on his hind legs, front paws in the air like a dancing bear, at any passing canine or lamb. Sometimes he mistakenly does this to me as I saunter past following the fun, but I rarely take part as I feel it is only for the young and easily pleased canines. He will get an embarrassingly quick smack down from me and soon enough will be off once again, galloping sideways with his back arched, ears flat against his head and tail all a squiggle, pretending he had intended to give me a fright and not in the least embarrassed by our brief fight. On sunny March days everyone enjoys these wanderings among the daffodil-flowered field.

There are many superstitions and old wives' tails (if you'll excuse the pun) that travel companionably through time and the history of farming. One of these is to see how the first ewe lambs down (one of many rural terms for a ewe giving birth to a lamb) at the beginning of the season. If it goes badly, there could be problems ahead, but if it goes well then the season might run its course relatively smoothly.

Not long ago we used to lamb in March. I remember the first ewes to lamb were from The Shepherd's old flock of mixed breeds. However, now, with lambing happening earlier in the year, I concentrate instead on making my morning rounds because egg-makers resume laying their eggs after a few months of winter rest. After hunting there is nothing that grabs me more than tracking down fresh raw warm eggs. Some crafty egg-makers hide their eggs, so I hunt for them in the clean loose piles of golden straw or aromatic hay in the sheep shed and stables. I descend behind and creep between large straw and hay bales. Once in a while I surprise a mouse or a rat to add to the fun when searching for my second breakfast of the day. I'm always ready to inform The Shepherd when I next see her and tell her all about my discovery while I march her to where I think egg nests are hidden. She collects and retrieves them, even if they've fallen behind bales of straw or hay. My scrumptious reward is a fresh raw egg. There's nothing I like better than an egg yolk. Eggs, eggs, glorious eggs … raw, scrambled, fried, but none better than farm-fresh raw eggs still warm from the nest.

I follow The Shepherd as she enters the stables to collect feed. I make sure to point out the bin containing our egg-makers' rolled barley. One scattered barley scoop is thrown every morning and they happily peck and scratch. After their barley breakfast, egg-makers head out to hunt for delectable insects, worms, grubs and seeds. They also graze on tasty grasses and delicious wild herbs that grow abundantly in our surrounding fields and which give their egg yokes a healthy, lovely deep rich orange colour and a unique gourmet flavour. Their yokes resemble the bright early-morning sun, which projects the arrival of a great day. In my feline mind, my gustatory opinion is that their diet makes eggs an obvious food to eat. A good healthy egg yolk is my favourite part of my favourite food, with the added benefit that it's great for my glossy fur coat. I can hear an eggshell crack from way across fields even when I am fast asleep in the sheep shed or stables. I arrive at a romping gallop, ears pricked forward, to wherever the cracked-egg noise came from. I've heard The Shepherd say that if you feed egg-makers food with a strong distinctive flavour like roast garlic or leftover Indian curry, that flavour will permeate the taste of eggs laid over the next few days. I must say this is very true indeed, but I personally prefer my eggs seasoned by our farm's insects, field grasses and wild herbs.

Every morning the four canines and I trot across the cobbled yard to a mesh-covered gate which has a vintage sign bolted to the stone pier right above where you open the gate. It states:

The gate must always be closed. If left open, the fine is forty shillings.

This sign is most important because it gives visiting strangers a laugh, so they pay attention to what it says despite its out-of-date numismatic fine. Shillings, pence and farthings have long gone but countryside golden rules prevail. A most important golden rule is that every gate you open to walk through must be closed behind you. Over the years members of my lovely flock of egg-makers have been killed by foxes, or once in a while by neighbours' dogs that strayed through an open gate. Both times the dogs were caught in the act and the neighbours paid for new egg-makers, BUT when foxes come calling, they usually slaughter all my egg-makers.

Late in March is when the 'kits' (the rural name for fox cubs) of our local mother fox (known as a vixen in our agrarian world) are old enough to start to need solid food. The mother will explore the countryside to find the most abundant food source to feed her hungry offspring. She will choose the easiest to take home. If the egg-makers are let out too early in the morning or the door to their house not tightly closed at night, the vixen will come and kill the whole flock, given half a chance. She will then bring one bird home to her kits and pull it apart to make it easy for them to eat bite-sized pieces. After she has fed her litter, she sneaks back as often as possible to retrieve as many of our egg-maker bodies as she can. The vixen trots off to a variety of locations in hedgerows or fields to bury egg-maker bodies. She uses the still-cool March earth as a storeroom, similar to a human's refrigerator, as a place to keep her extra food. She tries to do this in a timely way before The Shepherd or my canines discover the dead egg-makers.

Whenever we arrive and see what looks like wanton carnage, bloody bodies strewn across the egg-maker's paddock, The Shepherd becomes very upset. I sniff each body, make sure that it is dead and move on to examine the next. The canine work crew comes in, takes a quick note of the murdered egg-makers and then tactfully avoids even a passing glance at any egg-maker, dead or alive.

Their collective body language screams at The Shepherd: 'No, we did not do this, no, we did not do this, but we can smell a musky scent in the air.'

To each other: 'Can you smell that pungency?'

'Yes, quick, I got a whiff of that foxy musk. It seems to have gone this way.'

Turning to each other, the canines rush off, some with noses in the air and others with noses close to the ground, to follow the strong tang of fox scent. They collectively dash to a fresh hole dug recently under the egg-makers' fence to enter the kill zone. A few stray feathers would lie near the entrance dig or snagged in the fence wire, fluffed and wafting in the breeze. A trail of feathers is seen among the blades of grass and leaves or caught between sticks, all showing the vixen's passage across the field with her prized corpses.

Pepper usually leads my hunting pack as they follow an ambient whiff of fox musk that still hangs in the air. If The Shepherd sees our canine crew take off in a race across a field, she worries that the new tiny bat-like Puddlemaker Inca will get lost or killed in a fox or rabbit hole. I must confess I do admire the little dog's mighty tenacious attitude. She can provoke The Shepherd into a fit of giggles when she grabs Bear's tail and hangs on with a vice-like grip. She bounces behind, hanging on as Bear races after The Big Fellow. Both bigger dogs run shoulder to shoulder while they snap at each other in play. Bear's tail is the only one used by the Puddle-maker in her favourite game of 'Catch the Dragon's Tail'. The Puddlemaker hangs on till Bear's tail-feather hair suddenly gives way. When this happens Inca is sent flying and rolls over. She then scrambles up to race after both much bigger dogs, spitting out Bear's tail-feather hairs as she tries to catch another bouncing ride with her teeth. These shenanigans occur daily and sometimes Pepper deigns to takes part in this silly frolic of tomfoolery, much to my embarrassment.

On good days, when the flock has not been killed or eaten, the egg-makers are usually faffing about at the gate in antici-pation of breakfast. Sometimes the large cocky disruptive male, who's only good for making more egg-makers during the spring and summer months, perches high above my head on the gate and crows as if his life depends on it. I wait as

The Shepherd opens the gate to feed the egg-makers and I follow. As soon as barley grains hit the ground, I ask her to come with me into the egg-makers' house to see how many eggs have been left for me. I really get very annoyed when there are none.

Crows and magpies often fly into the egg-makers' house after they hear the happy clucks as one egg-maker successfully lays and then proudly struts away from her newly laid warm egg. I find this terribly foolish, advertising to the world that fresh eggs are available – it's practically inviting their foes into the nests to steal eggs. Occasionally, The Shepherd finds a trapped crow or magpie in the egg-makers' house when she's looking for eggs. From time to time a small wren, a robin or a sweet-singing blackbird is attracted by leftover barley. They hop through the small ground-floor egg-maker sized entrance. When they find themselves inside, they feel trapped and panic, having forgotten how they got in and unable to find a way out. When The Shepherd rescues these small birds, she releases them outside. They fly off slightly battered but essentially unharmed.

Once I saw the most beautiful bird of prey, a sparrowhawk, who had pursued a cheeky wren into the egg-makers' house through their small door, so promptly became trapped inside instead. A clever wren escaped through a wren-sized gap in the egg-makers' window, but the sparrowhawk wasn't so lucky. The Shepherd heard a clucking commotion when we came near the house, a noisy flapping and banging on windows. I knew right away that something larger than normal was caught inside, so I remained outside happily while The Shepherd dived in to try and catch the brown-and-white speckled sparrowhawk with her bare hands. The quicker she caught it, the less damage it was likely to do to itself by panicking in the confines of the enclosed space with its rack of roosting poles and nest boxes. When The Shepherd finally caught it, she brought it into the farmhouse for all of us to admire its beauty and stunning big yellow eyes. I padded behind and demanded that she reprimand it for scaring my egg-makers, who had broken their eggs and left a big eggy mess soaking into the wood shavings on the floor of their house, with not a decent egg left for me to eat.

Several egg-makers usually disappear in April or May. If they haven't been killed by a fox, they return in late May or June, leading troops of baby egg-makers behind them. They peck and chirp behind their mothers, who cluck around the yard, proudly showing off their newly hatched balls of multi-coloured fluff. I have to admit they can be quite sweet.

Mother egg-makers are very protective. I have seen them, wings out and spread feathers all fluffed up like a feather duster, chasing Ovenmitt across the yard, squawking and screaming at him to steer clear of their clutch of young. Ovenmitt has great respect for mother egg-makers, so much so that he will wait for me, The Shepherd or a canine to walk him past a mothering egg-maker. Even then he is very wary and if the egg-maker makes the slightest move towards him, even if only half fluffed up, Ovenmitt will skedaddle across the yard with his tail straight up in the air.

The Shepherd loves birds and often tells me the story of her favourite breakfast companion in Southeast Asia, a hornbill. (Incidentally, I'd like to mention to readers that my egg-makers originated in Asia. Wild egg-makers came from rainforests and were the first to be domesticated and bred. They became the many varieties of egg-maker that we have the world over today.) While The Shepherd was working for the wildlife charity in Southeast Asia, one of her jobs was to make a photographic record of the exercises that were needed to rehabilitate baby orangutans who had been taken into captivity by foolish humans and were crippled from having been fed incorrect foods in human homes. This rehabilitation centre was in Indonesia on the island of Java. It was essentially a kind of gentle physiotherapy for those poor primates. Every morning at breakfast The Shepherd's companion was a beautiful strange-looking jungle bird called a hornbill, whom she has described to me. He was a young male Knobbed Hornbill, sporting a black feathered body, which he held in an upright way, much like the Indian Runner duck, whom some of you will know due to his or her long neck and distinctive run.

The Shepherd's friend had a long feathery amber-coloured neck with beady eyes surrounded by pale blue skin, as if someone had smudged eyeshadow all around his eyes. His head actually looks like it was made up of an enormous beak, with a horn-like fixture on his crown that extended onto his huge bill. He waddle-walked around like a penguin and to get the measure of you, The Shepherd tells me, 'He would turn his head from side to side to peer at you.' But I still can't imagine what he'd look like with the illogical hodge-podge collection of odd animal parts she described.

He would sit on the table next to her while she ate breakfast and would ask for some of her fruit salad of grapes, mangoes and freshly picked bananas. This clever hornbill knew a soft touch when he saw one. The animal-loving Shepherd caved in so easily. She fed him one piece of fruit at a time by hand from her bowl until he'd had his fill. After he had taken the last piece he would clasp it in his magnificent beak and swallow it. Then he would toss his head, regurgitate the morsel of fruit unblemished and, with another small toss of his head, thoughtfully place the grape or piece of mango between the outmost tips of his ungainly beak to give it back to The Shepherd. She had to accept politely his regurgitated gift. Once the gift had been accepted, the hornbill would then grasp her hand gently in his large beak and hold it while she finished the rest of her breakfast one-handed. Once finished, she would stroke the back of the hornbill's soft feathery head. Honestly, if only I received anything like this same attention …

The one time that I have The Shepherd's undivided attention is when we take one of our working walks over Black Sheep Farm in search of the best nettle patch to harvest. Wild nettles are a spring tonic for our farm's grazers because their deep taproots pull all sorts of essential vitamins and minerals from our rich soil. Nettles are not foolish plants by any stretch of the imagination since they always choose the best, richest soil to grow in. Even when horses have a nice mineral lick, they will dig for nettle roots in winter. All our herbivores eat nettles once they are cut and left to dry for at least three days, which takes the sting out of them. The Shepherd cooks the nettles in stock made from the bones of home-cooked roast chicken.

I am always on hand when a chicken carcass is stripped before it is boiled into soup stock. We all stand about or sit in a row: Pepper, The Big Fellow, Bear, the new Puddle-maker, Miss Marley, Ovenmitt and I. We each wait our turn to get our morsel of chicken although I sometimes sink my claws into the hand that tenders the chicken morsel as it can be very slow coming round to my turn. It really is hard being a cat sometimes.

2
Sun and Showers

As March becomes April, The Shepherd keeps a close eye on the leaf buds as they swell on the oak and ash trees, since they are an age-old predictor of summer weather. This ditty surfaces every year, she tells me:

Oak before ash, we are in for a splash,
Ash before oak, we are in for a soak.

So every morning leaf buds are inspected and compared between these two species.

While daffodils still bloom in the fields, the grass, wild herbs and flowers really start to grow in the milder weather. The edges of the fields begin to prick out in many colours as the muddy month of March fades. The subtle pale greens of lords and ladies appear, celandine yellows the bottom of hedgerows with its rich egg-yoke flowers, while pale yellow primroses appear on banks and dog violets spread purple under trees, their colours deepening as the trees' leaves unfurl and shadow them. The fields are covered in strong yellow dandelions all humming with bees and other pollinating insects as they have their first good feed on blossoms after a long winter's hibernation. Cowslips burst up and out of their flat-lying leafy rosettes with pale yellow bells bobbing on any hint of wind. No longer are they picked to make cowslip wine, as they are a rare sight to behold in any quantity. Speedwell and vetches, blue and purple, add flashes of stippled colour through grasses as they flower. The Shepherd loves to eat vetch flowers as they taste like nutty flavoured green garden peas, and they add flavour and a beautiful colour to a fresh spring green salad. Rabbit food to me, but some humans are mad keen on their salad greens.

As flowers burst out and mild southwest winds blow in to warm the earth, young lambs frolic and cavort around trees or play a game of 'King of the Log' atop a fallen tree from a recent winter storm. I find the most transfixing to watch is a whole flock of lambs, who race to see who is fastest up a hilltop. They turn as if at an invisible marker, then with tails spinning like speed-inducing propellers, they race downhill in great leaps with a flourishing bouncing twist, which shows how healthy and happy they are.

Often while we watch these lambs' skylarking romps, the canine crew follow The Shepherd in a slow procession. Pepper watches with disinterested, amused tolerance, The Big Fellow is watchful for any mishaps that might occur and ready to step in as a concerned caretaker, while silly Bear trails behind with a look of longing, wanting to join in the fun they all seem to be having without him.

The collection of nettle leaves will form part of a delicious seasonal vegetable dish for the household of humans. I have no real interest in nettles. We cats find most vegetables dull compared to a tasty morsel of chicken, or a nice fresh mouse. Intermittently I will partake of a green bean, or some spears of grass I personally pluck to alleviate and dislodge an occasional hairball. Once nettles are cooked their sting is nullified and the resulting simple dish of nettle leaves steamed like spinach is served with a knob of butter, which The Shepherd tells me is scrumptious. However, I much prefer when The Shepherd makes nettle soup, because she uses stock made from the boiled bones from the Sunday lunch of roast chicken. The carcass has been steeped overnight in the simmering oven of the Aga with extra seasoning and chunks of carrots and onions, filling the kitchen with a delicious aroma. She then drains the chicken stock and to it, adds our fresh picked nettles with diced potatoes, boiled until they are soft. Then she whizzes with a very noisy whizzy machine till it's smooth. She adds some frozen green peas, stirs them in while reheating it only briefly so the peas still have a nice pop when crushed between the teeth. She then serves it with a good scrape of fresh nutmeg on top and if she's feeling really fancy a spoonful of crème fraîche or a nice dollop of Velvet Cloud sheep-milk yogurt. She talks a lot about the vitamins and minerals in the soup, and I pretend to listen, but really I'm only interested because it smells of chicken.

The Shepherd has not always been an expert in the kitchen, it has to be said. Long before I came here, in The Shepherd's distant youth she decided to dye some white trousers black. It was the most inexpensive way to get an article of seemingly new clothing. She bought the dye and asked her granny which pot she could use in the kitchen to boil water to dye the trousers. Her granny often used a big pot to cook dog food, which was made up of cheap scrap meats from the butcher. The meat was called offal or 'lights' and was usually mixed with lungs, tripe, sheep heads and cow stomachs. Puuurrsonally, I prefer The Shepherd's proffered raw liver and heart chunks. Her granny would cook this mix slowly in the Aga overnight. It filled the house with a distinctly different odour from that of stew or roast meat. This canine cookery event happened at least twice a week. Once the meat mix was cooked, it was removed to the meat safe just outside the kitchen door, which got little sun and where it perfumed the air in the scullery. The meat safe was an open wooden-shelved structure covered with fine metal mesh and it had a tall latched door to lock it. They were commonly used before refrigerators were invented. In fact, The Shepherd often tells me that the farmhouse's first refrigerator was rented and it was just a very small white box. The deep freeze proved to be a more useful purchase for her thrifty grandmother: it froze fruit for jam-making and blanched vegetables, which was how The Shepherd's granny and grandpa extended their season of dining on homegrown produce. Whenever there was over-production of garden fruit and veg, they also saved it to sell as well as for future household use.

Back to dyeing The Shepherd's white trousers … Granny had said that she could use the dog food pot between her stewing sessions for the canines. But this was impossible since The Shepherd planned to go out wearing the dyed black trousers the very next evening and she had found the pot of homemade dog food still quite full. There was another giant pot that was used to make jam or to boil ham and tongue for the human household to eat. The Shepherd thought this would be fine for her to use as long as she cleaned it well after use. So she worked away dyeing her white trousers black. She stirred the big boiling pot of white trousers and black dye on the Aga's hottest burner. When she had finished, she scrubbed the pot clean, or so she thought, and pronounced herself very pleased with a job well done. A few days later, her granny placed a ham in the big pot to boil for lunch that day. The boiled ham emerged coloured a deep indigo, much to the fury of The Shepherd's granny. Lunch that day was a very quiet meal as they all munched on indigo ham. Luckily, there were no guests on that day, or indeed on the succeeding days until they had consumed the whole ham.

I find April a great deal more annoying, because of horse chestnut trees. Just before their leaves unfurl in spring, the horse chestnut release a sticky sap, which covers its leaf-bud protectors. They fall to the ground, then seem to love to get caught up in my fine coat. I spend hours trying to rid myself of these sap-covered bud protectors, often only making it worse as I pull them off, unintentionally spreading the stickiness, so my coat becomes such a tangle that mats form. I then resign myself to the hands of The Shepherd to untangle my mats and comb out my fine hair. She has said this reminds her of times when she worked for the wildlife charity twenty-six years ago, when she watched geckos or lizards as well as big Komodo dragons. How she makes the connection I just don't know, but it seems when lizards lick their faces and clean their eyes, the way their tongue moves across their face seems like their tongue is sticky but in reality it's quite smooth.

The Shepherd describes once when the call of nature awoke her in the middle of the night when she was doing fieldwork in Malaysia. Not being able to find her torch, she had to feel her way along the walls to the bathroom. She takes particular delight in describing the hole in the floor that was their litter box – I have no idea why – but on this night, just as she was feeling her way down the steps to the litter box, a gecko jumped onto her face and ran across it, its cool little feet sticking to her skin like miniature suction cups, before leaping onto the opposite wall. Luckily, she didn't jump in fright or she might have fallen down steps into a deep mucky hole. I tolerate this and other stories as they seem to give her such amusement while she grooms annoying tangles out of my magnificent coat.

As April wears on, flowers spring up and bring in a second flush of colour to the fields around the farm. Cowslips, once a rare sight, pop out of their ground hugging leafy rosettes on slender stems with yellow clustered bells hanging, heads bobbing about in gusty spring breezes. The cuckoo flower's delicate pink blossoms signal the return migration of the irresponsible cuckoo bird. The cuckoo lays her eggs in another bird's nest, forcing her to raise the interloper that will result. Then the growing cuckoo chick pushes all of the natural chicks out of the nest. Cuckoos have a distinctive call and in springtime, 'cuckoo, cuckoo' can be heard across the fields and in the hedgerows. Sadly, the call is rarely heard any more when this flower blooms, because the modern farm practice of square-cutting hedges in winter means that the nest sites that small birds use – and that the cuckoo loves to invade – are fewer. With magpies able to find more exposed, less hidden nests and eat eggs or young hatchlings, even the cuckoo has less chance of survival.

Dandelions bloom in profusion and feed a hungry multiplicity of humming pollinators. Forget-me-nots flush blue, as does the delicate bloom of speedwell as it sprinkles its colour through the fresh spring green of growing grass. The Shepherd's favourites are blue wood anemones, with their ground covering profusion of blue stars, each with a cluster of white stamens at the centre. A proverbial sea of purple-blue spreads out under horse chestnut trees outside the kitchen window. They were planted by The Shepherd's grandmother, who loved flowers.

As spring awakens, it brings with its floral bounty parasites that love to prey on lambs. Ewes have to be brought in to queue up in our sheep yard, along with their lambs, who get their first worm dose, which will be particularly needed if spring has been mild and wet. Some years lambs are fine and need no worm dose. Other years they'll need several doses if the ground is very moist. There are a large variety of worms, ranging from those who are productive builders of soil to the few that prey on the internal organs and digestive systems of animals. An infestation of parasitic worms among sheep can spread very quickly; if not dealt with, lambs can die or never fully recover their zest for life. Essentially a parasitic worm's survival is down to its ability to leech out all the vitamin, mineral and protein goodness in a ewe's milk. The fresh new grass meant to give a lamb healthy growth also becomes a hazard. A parasitic worm's life cycle is ruthlessly efficient: sheep consume mature eggs from grass they graze. These worm eggs incubate, hatch, ingest parasitically from the sheep's insides, then lay thousands of eggs, which are pooped out into grass for the next sheep to eat.

To prevent this happening, The Shepherd and I walk the fields every day, weaving our way through our flock of ewes and lambs. While canines lack interest – all rush off to chase a squirrel, rabbit or hare – I walk among the sheep. Lambs snooze like cats in what The Shepherd sees as a most uncomfortable position with their little heads at strange, almost impossible angles. We walk around making sure that we have seen every single lamb stand up and move around. We try to wake them as gently as possible whenever we examine them. The best way for us to tell if lambs look well in themselves is to see if they have a good long stretch. Their fine necks and backs arch like a cat after a good nap and they stretch their tail straight up in the air with a little wiggle at the end.

I always love these spring walks through our fields with The Shepherd, old meadows coming to life with early flowers in bloom feeding hungry early pollinating insects, which hum all around, birds singing and flitting about collecting food for young chicks. One hopes the worst of the winter has been left behind as days grow longer and nights shorter. Throughout April The Shepherd keeps an eye out for our annual migrants, the birds who return to repair, rebuild or build new nests in the barns and sheds. We like how the swallows feed on pests and insects, which will have started to annoy sheep in the evenings or early mornings.

When our swallows arrive home to Ireland it usually bodes well as they glide in on a bow wave of a front of warm weather. When they first arrive they're often exhausted and swoop in to land on overhanging cables, their excited chitter-chatter filling the air. This is also when The Shepherd shakes her finger at myself, Ovenmitt and Miss Marley, giving us all a stern lecture about not catching, killing or tormenting our visiting long-distance travellers. One of us usually fails at this when a tired swallow glides in too slow and too low. With an athletic twisting leap from one of us, the demise is quick. Later, when swallow chicks are close to fledging out, and readying themselves for their first flights across the yard, we find our way across hazardous as swallows dive-bomb, peck and torment us.

At night, birds still hungry from winter sit on their recently built nests to incubate their first batch of eggs. Luckily, they cannot see their hermaphrodite neighbours, the worms, come out to dance a sensual reproductive ballet among themselves. When soil softens after rain I can hear worms disconnect from each other to slip back into their holes to avoid being trodden on as I pad over their kingdom of rich soil. Sometimes when The Shepherd walks across a field by torchlight to check on a lamb or sheep, her beam of light illuminates the worms vulnerable above ground. It's not the light that disturbs them, but her footsteps vibrating through the ground a ripple that disturbs the cavorting worms, who rapidly withdraw back into their holes in the ground.

At this time of year, if we haven't done so in autumn, we spread granulated lime over fields that need their acid pH brought up to a neutral level (more about this later) to grow grass well. This farm job is one in which our preparation and clean-up take the most time, as our equipment must be cleaned after use to keep lime and condensation from corroding the metal bits of our spreader and seizing up the working parts. When The Shepherd races around the fields on the quad towing the spreader to scatter the lime granules, Pepper loves to ride behind her on the quad's rear end, watching out for a rabbit or squirrel to chase. I, however, usually hop on board for a spin up to the yard when The Shepherd has stopped the quad and dismounted at a gate to open it. Pepper and I then share the ride, me up front on the warm engine cover, while he stands behind The Shepherd.

In May, what we call 'fairies' dance in the long, low evening light above the sheep's heads, beneath the branches of the larch trees. These insects, with their long transparent wings, are called lacewings, The Shepherd tells me. They are my favourite May event, apart from the newly risen cow parsley, the king of wild flowers, which blossoms in our woods and shady hedgerows in May. It towers above me as I stroll behind The Shepherd and wend my way through their forest of green stems. A sea of white lacy blossom floats above me as dappled sunlight seeps through the thickening tree canopy above us. Our sheep love to munch on cow parsley leaves and savour their flowery heads. They rub their heads and bodies against the stems to break them apart and cover themselves with parsley juice. Wise sheep do this because they've learned that cow parsley juice naturally repels annoying flies. So, when the sheep are let into fresh pasture, they race to wherever cow parsley grows. They munch it and rub themselves thoroughly until only a few stubby stems remain. Despite this annual abuse by my sheep, cow parsley has a deep vigorous root which enables its return every year as long as a percentage of its leafy greens get to feed and store its needs with enough sunlight.

When I first came to Black Sheep Farm all those years ago, I apprenticed myself to the worldly old feline Oscar. Oscar taught me everything I know. In those days, well before I came to take over, there were no sheep on The Shepherd's farm. Wildlife, Terrier Tassie, and cats Tabitha and Tina occupied the territory. A farmer rented our fields to graze cattle eleven months of the year. Then, when Oscar was a teenager, The Shepherd was given a few orphaned lambs from whom we'll call the curly-haired sheep farmer, a friendly neighbour whom she had known since they were children. Back then she could not afford to buy sheep to breed. She made a pen from wooden pallets. At lambing time she found straw and borrowed a heat lamp. She collected small plastic drink bottles, bought a rubber nipple to fit them, and bought artificial sheep milk. Oscar then and there decided that it was his first duty to help keep the lambs warm under the heat lamp and secondly to clean their faces after they had finished each milky bottle-feed. He carefully attended orphan lambs, especially when the heat lamp was on. I'm told the humans sometimes couldn't tell what was cat and what was lamb in the pile of small bodies asleep under the lamp. Oscar loved to walk with the lambs. While they were his cat size or smaller, his tail often curled over their backs to reassure them as they followed The Shepherd outside the pen for the first time. During feeding time he sometimes flopped on his side and played with a lamb's tail. Their tails have a lively life as they suckle their mother ewes or lamb formula bottles. Tails spin and wriggle as the lambs' bellies fill with warm milk. At other times Oscar sat near the lambs' heads and leaned over to lick dribbles of milk that seeped between bottles and lamb lips as they suckled. Oscar was also a dedicated assistant gardener. He enjoyed nothing more than freshly dug rich earth for a good back roll. He diligently kept our Gardening Boss robin away from any worms that turned up in a recently dug flower bed.

Unlike me, Oscar's past is no mystery. He was born on a small farm in Curraheenavoher, near Ballymacarbry in the Nire Valley, County Waterford, in the foothills of the Comeragh Mountains. He came to Black Sheep Farm as a weaned kitten as there was a need for new blood to reduce an expanding rat and mouse population. The farm cats at that time were siblings Tabitha and Bettina, who was called Tina. They were The Old Guard felines from The Shepherd's grandparents' days. Both were aged happy cats. Tabitha was a plump tabby and loved a human lap, I am told. Tina was shy, lean and black. They arrived at our farm as kittens, having been thrown in a brown paper bag onto the road by some despicable human. The Shepherd's grandmother spoilt them rotten with saucers of milky tea and cuts of well-buttered toast. Neither cat had any interest in hunting unless an animal of prey variety literally fell into their laps – which is indeed what happened one day, The Shepherd tells me, in one of the stories she finds so amusing.

One day, as she sat at the kitchen window, fat Tabitha, in her elderly manner, lounged and dozed under a horse chestnut tree. While Tassie the Terrier snuffled in nearby grass, she unearthed a pheasant who had been crouched and thought itself hidden. It jumped up, raced around the tree, straight into sleeping Tabitha. Tabitha leapt up in shocked surprise, extended her claws and killed the bird in the blink of an eye. The Shepherd ran outside for a closer look. She saw Tabitha proudly drag her prey by its neck between her front legs to a secret location in order to privately partake of her surprise feast just as her wild panther cousin would.

Cat Oscar, on the other hand, had been raised as a kitten by his mother on fresh farmyard mouse meat and was therefore an excellent candidate for the role of rat-and-mouse-killer-cat. Oscar's calm easy-going demeanour belied a strong hunting instinct. He was not a chatty cat, but the strong silent type, who always purred steadily but quietly whenever he popped into a human's lap. What I most liked to do companionably with Oscar, other than to curl up with him on a cold winter's night in the stable hay for more warmth, was to hunt for rabbits. This was one of his favourite occupations, so I was very glad to be taught by such a keen expert.

However, I have to confess that from my beginnings at Black Sheep Farm I was a clumsy oaf. I constantly fouled up hunts with my naïve impatient enthusiasm. Often I leapt too soon. I foiled my catch because my hoped-for rabbit had ample time to escape with a powerful jump and twist in the air. Those rabbits avoided my premature leap of long forelegs and extended claws.

Our other hunting problem arose from my much-beloved Shepherd, who had given me such a lovely new life and home. She occasionally appeared out of the blue and made her way across our hunting field as we silently prowled towards our intended prey, rustling the grass and alerting the rabbit, which hopped quickly away to safety. Our hunts only became efficient after Oscar and I carefully demonstrated our techniques. To give her great credit The Shepherd stood statue still after that and carefully watched how we hunted. The excellent result was that she and we learned to understand each other much better.

A hunt would often start when we found ourselves of the same mind. We would move out to our favourite place, a long hedgerow in the uppermost hilltop field with lots of rabbit burrows along its western edge. Oscar had found this a perfect location, because the morning sun first lights the frosted grass in front of the rabbits' burrows, thawing the grass earliest in the cold of winter, so they like to graze there.

The field is named the Wind-Charger Field because long ago it had a windmill that spun to charge big batteries that provided electricity for Black Sheep farmhouse. When The Shepherd was small, her grandparents and mother told her about The Olden Days before and during the Second Big Human War, known as the Second World War, when the farmhouse was lit with candles and paraffin lamps. After the war ended, they built a windmill to generate electricity. This erratic form of electric current was totally wind dependent: as the wind varied, the lights flickered. The wind-charger's electricity lit the Black Sheep farmhouse until electric power mains were introduced into rural County Kilkenny in 1946. (These were our earliest days of making what is now considered alternative energy. Back then, fossil fuels were too expensive to use for making rural electricity. That's why candles, paraffin lamps and this early wind power were the most important sources of our indoor light in The Olden Days.) The wind-charger had been taken down before The Shepherd was born. Recently, she cleared out an old shed and found the long wooden propeller, covered in dust and generations of cobwebs, which had spun in winds to provide electricity so many years before.

But back to the hunting. Oscar and I would meet up in the small cobbled outer yard. I would follow him through what I called our 'gate squeeze', between the gatepost and pillar of the gate, which is fitted with a tight mesh. We'd slide through into the egg-maker's Plum Orchard paddock: in spring, after plum blossoms have faded, they fall and litter the ground with a dusting of pinky-white petals. We would saunter into the Wind-Charger paddock, a small fenced-off part of the great big field that we often use for sheep that need close observation. As we'd pass close to the lean-to shed where ewes birth lambs in winter and spring and are shorn during summer months, a swallow or two might dive-bomb us until we moved far enough away from their nests.

We'd wander slowly up the Wind-Charger Field, weave through a few beds of nettles, grass cool underfoot, clover soft on our pads, and we'd step around spiky thistles. Thistle thorns in our paws are incredibly painful, crippling even, so we always tried to avoid them. Having left the swallows behind us, we'd hope no corvids – magpie, raven, rook, jackdaw, carrion crow or even the grey crow, with its grey skull cap feathering – would spot us heading out to hunt and spoil our fun with their warning racket of cackle, caw and crow. We'd have to stop and pretend to clean our toes until they left to look for another distraction to scream about. As we headed up the hill, wagtails would bob about, snatching insects among the grasses, flit up to the tops of fence posts, or perch atop wire fences with tails wagging and heads bobbing as if to say: 'We see you and we are quite aware of your presence. Move along, move along. We need to get back to our business of hunting insects to feed our young. Move along, move along.'

Once we'd travelled far enough away from the sheltered nesting sites of the swallows, they would resume darting, diving, gliding after insects disturbed from the grass by our passing through. Out in the field they never flew low or close enough to enable us to leap and catch one of them for a tasty morsel. When and if we ever caught a swallow, it was usually in spring when they had just returned, exhausted from their marathon migration north to us from South Africa.

Oscar and I were lucky if we got past all the natural early-warning systems of other species and made it up to just below the brow of the Wind-Charger hill. There we'd pause to lower our bodies and flatten our ears sideways so their tips didn't break the horizon line and give our silent crouched-low position away. We'd cautiously peer over the field as it sloped down away from us. We remained stone-still, with only a telltale twitch of a tail to betray our presence. We'd watch a few rabbits grazing along the hedgerow – luckily, no russet-red hare could be seen. Hares are far more wary and attentive to our intentions than their cousin rabbits.

Early in our hunting relationship, I found it tedious and boring to wait for the correct moment to begin – sometimes I just sat bolt upright and scared rabbits away when my ears and head broke their visible horizon line of clean grassy hill. Oscar was very displeased with my impatient hunting behaviour and would give me a stern look.

As we crouched and watched rabbits move about, dining on our sheep's grass, we hoped no hungry hunting buzzard would coast overhead and spot our rabbit prey before we could try to catch it ourselves. Whenever we chose a rabbit to catch, we separated so that we could come at the creature in a pincer movement. Oscar usually swung out at a trot low to the ground in a big circle away from me and to the other side of our selected rabbit. Once in position, he aimed at the selected rabbit, flicked his tail as a signal to me and started his cautious prowl, ears flat, one calculated light step at a time. The tiny tip of his tail came to life under his concentrated pressure and flicked back and forth. I started my approach towards the rabbit from the other side, with the same concentrated vigilance, cautious with each step I took. Gingerly I placed each paw to advance by increments. At such a slow pace it seemed to me that time stretched out, slower and slower and longer and longer. If the wind wafted just the right way and no bird squawked a warning cry, we could draw closer to the end game.

In the beginning, before I learned properly, I would be the one to break first. Like the release from an over-wound spring, I would leap out from my low-crouched prowling stance to pounce. I'd bound through the gap that separated me from the rabbit. The rabbit would leap and twist in the air to evade me, most often fleeing directly towards Oscar, who had remained hidden in the long grass. He would leap into the air, claws full out, and bring down the rabbit, just like our lion cousins who dwell on the great plains of Africa. We would feast on scrumptious fresh rabbit and feel fat and lazy for days afterwards.

I miss Oscar terribly now he is gone as, although I have finally got the hang of it, I can only do my rabbit hunting in spring, when the rabbits are young and foolish. I haven't yet been able to train Miss Marley or Ovenmitt to hunt with such intelligent skill and cooperation as good old Oscar, although I hunt alone too, which, I have to admit, sometimes has its benefits.

3
Horses, Horses and More Horses

I cannot begin to tell you how much The Shepherd loves horses, from her earliest days as a child on Black Sheep Farm to her cousins' Maryland pony farm and to her schooldays, when she sought refuge from bullying by working at a local stable. There, she mucked out and cleaned the owners' stables and gave riding lessons to beginners. In exchange for her work she was allowed to ride horses. Later, while at agricultural college in America, she would work with draught horses – sometimes known as cart horses – in Vermont; she would break and train Morgan horses, a popular American breed, in upstate New York, and later still, she would ride in the Blue Ridge Mountains of Virginia, which are so like our own Irish Blackstairs Mountains that we can see from our farm's upper fields. Caring for and riding horses enabled her to develop and hone her skills at reading the unspoken language of the body that communicates across species, within herds and between prey and predator animals.

Each species communicates among themselves using its own unique language. But with our body language we can cross-communicate between species. All humans must long ago have had the innate ability to read animal body language in order to survive, but lost that skill as they left the natural world further and further behind. I know that The Shepherd has an instinctive understanding of how to communicate with us, and she can work real magic with horses. In America, as her skills with animals grew, she became accomplished at schooling difficult horses. She would create a rapport calmly with the animal to motivate the horse to obey rather than to force it and she could sense how and when to nudge it gently to bring forth its abilities. She tells me that she would often lose herself in concentration while riding a young horse.

When I first arrived at Black Sheep Farm, there was a mare who lived on the farm named Major Beth. She was a grey mare, half Connemara pony and half thoroughbred. She was tall enough at fifteen and a half human hands, or sixty-two inches. (For those of you who may not know, a horse's height is measured from the bottom of the front hooves to the 'withers', which are at the base of the neck. Each hand measure is four inches – the average size of a man's hand.) Major Beth was the first horse The Shepherd had ever owned outright. Previously she had just borrowed horses or owned only part of a horse.

Last, but far from least, is the black pony, Marco Polo, who I also met when I first arrived at the farm. Like me, he has a fascinating rescue story that profoundly improved his life. Of course, I found many of us on our farm had had phenomenal escapes and rescues thanks to The Shepherd. Even when she was elsewhere, in the bustle of New York City during the 1980s when she was learning the ropes in the theatre, or later in London, she found herself drawn to animals. In London, she regularly exercised a beautiful bay thoroughbred gelding that lived at Kentish Town City Farm. The only drawback to this arrangement was having to ride the horse before 6.30 a.m. to avoid London's rush-hour traffic, which would make the streets impassable for The Shepherd and her borrowed horse. The Shepherd would get up at 4 a.m. and walk from her flat in South Hill Park and then walk across Hampstead Heath to the City Farm. After unlocking the farm gate she would tack up the horse and ride along quiet London streets back up to Hampstead Heath.

One of her most memorable rides, she tells me, took place on a chilly, foggy autumnal morning. As she rode from the farm gates, the horse's hooves clip-clopped in muffled echoes as they moved along mist-shrouded streets. The fog eddied and flowed around and over them as if they waded through streaming liquid. Traffic lights appeared as dimly coloured glows through silver mist that slowly brightened as she drew nearer. The few early cars out and about drove slowly and cautiously.

When they arrived at Hampstead Heath, horse and rider entered a fairyland, as the heath's trees, clothed in autumn reds and golden yellows fringed with faded greens and dark browns, were veiled in shrouds of mist. They moved into the park's obscure stillness at a brisk trot and as they did so, they heard a bagpipe faintly humming in the distance. When they came to the spot where they always began to canter up the centre of the park, The Shepherd squeezed her legs to ask the horse to gallop. They flew up the hill, hoof beats now a muted clatter on the path, mist swirling about both horse and rider. Both invigorated by their speed uphill and across open land, they penetrated a dark stand of forest. The far-off bagpipe grew louder, so they slowed to a collected canter. Suddenly they emerged from the dark wood into a small glade, mist swirling around them. They surprised the man who played his bagpipes. He had obviously chosen this woodland glade in which to practise as it was as far away as he could get from sleeping Londoners. The horse smoothly rocked the rider back and forth, very slowly prancing at the canter. He almost danced to the bagpiper's marching tune, waited for the music to change to martial and readied himself for a cavalry charge towards enemies hidden among the wooded glade's mist-shrouded trees. The piper played on and bowed his head to acknowledge a unique shared moment with horse and rider. He probably had not heard the galloping hooves over the musical sounds of his humming pipes. As The Shepherd rode back to the City Farm, she felt exuberant and recharged by her exceptional early morning adventure. She thrived on that day's thrills for months afterwards.

Returning to Marco Polo, The Shepherd had put the word out that she was looking for a companion animal for Major Beth. A friend got in touch with her and said he might have the perfect companion, a nice-looking small black Welsh Mountain pony. The only problem was that he was still a stallion. Just a few weeks earlier our pony's rescuer, a farmer who lived on a less-travelled road – let's call him the Gentle Man, as he would be embarrassed if we drew more attention to him – had noticed him, small and hungry, wandering the roads wearily and grazing edges and hedges. One day, as he passed the place where the pony usually nibbled, he saw a group of men trying to catch him. They tried to corner him but he always escaped at a fast gallop, head low, so no thrown rope could catch him, with a buck and a swish of his tail. Our Gentle Man was amused and secretly hoped the wee pony would continue to escape, since he knew from their distinctive overalls where those men worked. The meat factory just up the road round the corner on the hillside took in horses from all over the countryside, slaughtered them and made their meat into dog food.

The next day the wee black pony, still on the loose, munched as much roadside grass as he could chew before someone tried to catch him again. But now he grazed very close to the Gentle Man's small farm. So out on the road the farmer went, opened a gate to his fields, shook the ever-magic bucket of sweet feed and persuaded the pony to enter one of his fields. When he looked closely at the pony he discovered that the little fellow had great raw wounds around his neck. They looked as if a rope had been tied around his neck so tightly that it had rubbed deep wounds through his skin and into the muscles of his neck. To this day you can still see his scars, because white hairs grew to cover his injured skin and muscle instead of his own natural black. If you run your paw across these white strips of pony hair, you can feel a hard scarred dip where the rope rubbed deep into his neck.

This Gentle Man was not only a farmer but also an expert on horses and an excellent breeder of Connemara ponies. He thought the little black pony was a thoroughbred Welsh Mountain stallion. He felt that he might have been stolen from a Welsh pony breeder in England or Wales and then brought to Ireland to sell as a children's pony. The pony was probably much too spirited for a child, so the people who owned him tried to starve him into submission. The Gentle

Man suspected that the pony never quieted enough, so the owner sold him to the horse-meat factory to try to make a bit of money. Luckily, the clever boy escaped.

By the time The Shepherd came back to her friend's farm to see how this little black pony was getting on, his neck wounds had nearly healed. She fell in love with him immediately, so the farmer agreed to keep the pony until he had finished healing and he had castrated him.

When Marco Polo finally came home to Black Sheep Farm his lively spirit had returned. He had a glossy black coat, a thick long flowing black tail and mane, a white blaze that was broad on his forehead and narrowed down to a snip on his soft black muzzle, a few white spots around his hooves, and white streaks on his neck over the rope scars. Right away he became a great companion for Major Beth. Even when The Shepherd rode off on Major Beth, Marco Polo never complained about being left alone.

As filaments of time wove their strands together, The Shepherd discovered more gossamer threads to weave into Marco Polo's story. He hated young human boys, so she assumed he had been beaten by boys trying to ride him into submission. Later on, she took Marco Polo to a man who trained horses to pull carts and traps to see if she could drive him harnessed to a cart. Marco Polo took to drawing a small cart like a cat drawn to a wool blanket on a cold wet day. The man said he must have once been very well trained for driving. He moved out with only a tongue-cluck, responded to a light touch on the reins, and could turn left or right properly, crossing over his legs easily.

The Shepherd and Marco Polo became a great team. She drove him along local roads and he competed in driving competitions at dressage venues, where he won award ribbons. They worked in movies together and modelled for students in art classes. Once the pair trotted six miles from the home farm to Thomastown, where they strolled into Carroll's Pub. There, she unhitched him from the cart and led him inside. Marco Polo's iron-shod hooves clip-clopped along the lovely flagstones of the long limestone corridor. Two men who were sat chatting animatedly in the pub abruptly froze silent to listen. When Marco Polo and The Shepherd appeared round the corner the men heaved sighs of relief. One of them exclaimed, 'Thank God! I thought I'd too much drink taken and was hearing things. Thank God 'twas a real horse and not the devil playing on my mind.' Relieved, they laughed uproariously.

Another pub visit found Marco Polo and The Shepherd in another Thomastown hostelry, The Bridge Brook Arms, after they had had a perfect wintry day driving about. The back of this tall, white-painted pub, with its black shutters, had an outdoor smoking area with a tented roof and an open fire for cold days. A group of friends had gathered round the fire to chat and enjoy each other's company in the warm glow. One friend brought Marco Polo a bag of carrots, which he quietly munched. A second held a pint of Guinness for him. When yet another friend arrived, he approached the talkative group, joined the conversation, walked past Marco Polo, stopped at his shoulder and absent-mindedly placed his hand down on Marco Polo's withers. He began to stroke him, chatting and laughing with everyone else. Marco Polo always behaved fine when he was touched as long as The Shepherd stood right next to him. However, as he was wont to do when standing still for a while, he adjusted his back legs and leaned down to scratch his knee. With a shout, the new visitor leapt backwards in fright. He turned white as a sheet … 'What the f**k!' He'd never noticed the black pony at the fireside. A friend exclaimed: 'This black lump of a pony has been here since before you came in and you didn't even notice him!'

As the years flew by The Shepherd bought Silver, an Irish draught mare. Both Major Beth and Silver birthed attractive foals, whom The Shepherd was able to sell to caring individuals she knew. This increased our farm's meagre income. She loved foaling time, as did I, because it meant lots of late-night company in the stables. I helped with foal birthing, although I found it a bit more complex than birthing sheep because foals and mares are so much bigger than lambs and ewes. As with my lambing, whenever long pauses occurred during foal birthing I sniffed and prowled my way silently through nearby hay or straw to hunt and snap up a mouse or rat.

Foaling Major Beth reminds me of the time when The Shepherd used to smoke. This might seem like a bit of a leap to you, but there is a connection. The Shepherd launched on tobacco in her early twenties while she was modelling, acting and working as a backstage hand in theatres, and as a bartender in New York City. Surrounded by smokers she took to inhaling cigarettes as a way to while away time among her friends, most of whom smoked. Years later, she became a dab hand at rolling her own cigarettes with one hand while riding a horse on long treks through the forests of Virginia's Blue Ridge Mountains. The Shepherd was quite pleased with herself for this bizarre accomplishment, even if her brown leather riding chaps had small grey and black stains all over them. She never flicked hot cigarette ash in the forest for fear of starting forest fires on hot dry summer months. To prevent any hot ash from falling onto the dry forest floor she would roll the spent grey cigarette ash along the upper inside of her chaps. When she had smoked her cigarette she would stub it out on her chaps.

For many years, she alternated between smoking and quitting smoking. Eventually she decided enough was enough when she realised how much she spent on something that just went up in smoke. The year she quit, The Shepherd had three foals about to drop: Silver, Major Beth and a new mare she had bought in foal. She recognised that she would get very little sleep and would have no cigarettes either to mitigate the foul moods due to her sleep deprivation, so, three months before foaling time, she bought a pack of smokes and opened them to make sure they became nasty and stale by the time foaling time rolled around. She then invested in little shots of fruit and vegetable juices so that whenever her tobacco addiction plagued her, she gulped a tot of healthy fruit or vegetable drink instead.

I once tried one and was disgusted. I suppose since I'm purely carnivorous that prevents me from enjoying such a cocktail. She enjoyed her vegetable and fruit treats and indeed they worked so well that Oscar and I never had the nasty smell of used tobacco smoke in our fur coats again. Our hunting became much more expedient. When we had smelly smoky coats, our dingy tobacco perfume frightened rabbits away if the wind changed direction and wafted our accumulated smoke-permeated scent towards them and they thought a human was close by.

Major Beth had her first foal in May during the time that The Shepherd quit her smoking habit. She had a bay filly, the first foal to be born on Black Sheep Farm since before The Shepherd was born.

For the first two days of their lives, foals are still very wobbly on their pins as they find out how their legs work;

they sleep a lot, eat and stay close to their mare mother. By the third day they have got a handle on early life and begin to gallop, but they still have a big problem: they don't know how to put on the brakes. Their long spidery legs carry them rapidly forward across the ground till they decide to stop, when they try their front brakes, only to fall over in a heap onto their noses. They untangle their legs, stand up slightly, nonplussed, and take off again. This time they apply their rear brakes only to land on their bottoms with a look of surprised embarrassment. Standing up once more with some energetic tail swishes, they trot off pretending that their crashes never happened.

During the third day of Major Beth's first foal's life, The Shepherd went out to see how the foal was getting on. When she arrived in the stonewalled paddock, all The Shepherd could see was Major Beth trotting about nickering in a very worried fashion. There was no sign of the filly foal anywhere. Where could it have gone? The walled garden paddock was very small at half an acre, the walls on three sides at least fifteen feet high and its gates over four feet tall with no space under them for a foal to roll out by mistake. The fence along the fourth side of the small paddock had no hole in it that a foal could fit through. The Shepherd started to walk along the edge of the wall, thinking the foal was lying flat on its side in a dip of the ground and somehow the mare had misplaced it. As The Shepherd walked on, she approached an old deep cement water tank that was filled from an aquifer that arose beneath the wall. As she approached she could make out a pair of ears sticking up just above the wall of the tank. She rushed forward to find an exhausted filly completely immersed in water except for her head, which she gamely managed to hold just above the water with her nostrils scrunched up to keep water out. The foal was barely alive.

With super-human strength, The Shepherd pulled the filly out of the water tank. She stripped off the sweater she had worn on that chilly May day and began to rub it vigorously over the foal's shivering cold body. The Shepherd put her fingers into the filly's mouth only to discover that it was very cold, a terribly bad sign that the filly was in shock and hypothermic. Major Beth was nickering, nudging, biting the filly's ears and pawing with her hoof at her cold body, urging her to stand up. As soon as Major Beth and The Shepherd got the filly to stand between them, the mare on one side and The Shepherd on the other, The Shepherd half-carrying the shivering filly, they moved the wobbly foal down to the yard into a straw-filled stable away from the chill wind of early May.

Once The Shepherd dared to stop rubbing the filly for five minutes, she ran into the house to phone the vet on the landline. (In those days she did not own a mobile phone and few people did.) I sat vigil on the window ledge in the stable and gave the occasional bit of advice as The Shepherd worked hard to warm up the filly. Later that night, after the filly had been saved with help and advice from the vet, The Shepherd decided to christen her with the Irish name Uisce, which means 'water'. The Shepherd spells it phonetically, Ishka, so those not versed in the Irish language can pronounce it correctly.

Ishka recovered fully and still lives on Black Sheep Farm. She birthed her own daughter, a beautiful bay called Grasshopper, several years ago. Sadly for us all, a few years after Ishka was born, Major Beth came down with cancer and had to be put to sleep. Two years later, Silver was in such immense pain in her knees from arthritis that she also had to be put to sleep humanely. So now just three equines remain: handsome Ishka, her lovely daughter Grasshopper and the ever-resplendent Marco Polo. Oh yes, and the water tank now has a lid across most of it, with just a gap left for animals to drink from, so this kind of event shall not happen again.

Part II
SUMMER

4

Hay Heat of June

In early summer, people come to buy our lambs after they are weaned from their mother ewes. The Shepherd and I then walk the fields to assess the lambs to see how they are growing and to estimate when they will be ready to go to new homes. We bring the flock into the yard, where she sorts and loads weaned ewe lambs to go to new breeders, and the wethers to smallholders. (Wethers are castrated male lambs, grown to be harvested for meat when they nearly approach full adult size.) Zwartbles sheep are unique in that they mature slowly. It takes eight to ten months for them to gain enough weight for harvest. Standard commercial sheep bred only for meat mature much faster. Their age is similar to feline years, so in estimated comparison to human years the wethers are about eighteen years old. This ovine age comparison can vary depending on sheep breed, similar to how some large dog breeds do not live as long as some of the smaller ones. 'Tis of course universally known that the vast majority of felines live longer than the average canine. Some might quote Philip Stanhope to you: 'A novel must be exceptionally good to live as long as the average cat.' But I choose to think he must be referring to an exceptionally bad version of *War and Peace* or *The Mahabharata*.

When the sun arrives at its June zenith in the northern hemisphere, it is a tower of solar heat and may melt the best of us. I still work away at my usual labours. First, I do my early-morning rounds, walking our fields to count legs and divide by four before the sun's heat grows too great. Secondly, after my breakfast, I sometimes go straight out into the garden to find a lovely cool spot under a box hedge, shrub or among tall euphorbia plants. I like places that have recently been weeded or dug over, as freshly turned earth is so cool. I snooze while a background buzz of pollinators fills the air with productivity.

One May morning, I had taken up my usual position and The Shepherd had just walked past, bade me good morning and continued on her way to check on the ewes and lambs. As I lay there the soil around me warmed as the sun rose. I slowly came to the realisation that something was tickling under me. I lay back and rolled about and hoped that would adjust whatever had lightly tugged at my fur. As I put my head upon the ground I heard a tiny scratching sound near my ear. I turned and perked up my head to peer as a tiny amount of soil began to rise upwards. I sat up to look down and readied myself to pounce if this was a mouse, vole or shrew about to erupt out of the ground. Instead a tiny black head with twitching antennas worked its way up out of the dry soil. A little bee emerged with a beautiful rich foxy-red hairy back. She diligently pushed away soil. It seems I had unintentionally blocked the entrance to her nest. As I got up and looked around more closely, I saw the ground was pocked with tiny granular piles around small holes. As I watched, more and more black heads with furry red bodies emerged into the morning sun. That marked the end of my morning snooze in that particular spot. It was a most educational moment for me when I learned that some species of bees live underground while other sorts live as a community in hives. I later discovered that these burrowers are called tawny mining bees, which were thought extinct until The Shepherd informed Biodiversity Ireland that we had loads popping out of the ground here. Still, nature never ceases to surprise me.

After The Shepherd and I have scrutinised the weather forecasts closely and think rain is not threatening, we decide it's time to make hay. Beautiful long grasses with full seed heads, clovers, vetches and herbs must be mown. Ideally we need ten days of good weather to make sure the grass to be cut and made into hay has adequate time for full prepara-tion. When grass is first mown it must lie for a day or two, then be spun out with a machine called a tedder, a very scary-looking rotating set of prongs, to dry.

We hope for a good crop of hay. The earlier we mow the grass with its big seed heads and the quicker it dries, the quicker it then becomes delicious hay with increased protein content. Retention of protein means better hay for sheep, who will enjoy it and remain healthier throughout the cold winter months.

When The Shepherd turns us felines out of the kitchen, I find hay's scent of summer absolutely wonderful. 'Tis so pleasantly soporific that I sleep very well indeed. I even dream of the mice and rats I hope to catch when I awaken. What's more, there is nothing like hay's warmth, which greatly comforts all three of us cats while it's cold outside.

I stay well clear of machinery when grass is being mown for hay. After the mowing I walk with The Shepherd through the freshly cut grass. She hunts for any ragweed or thistles she might have missed before it was mowed. Ragweed poisons horses and cattle. Thistles and thorns may pierce The Shepherd's gloves and prick painful holes in her hands whenever she draws hay from a bale in winter.

I always look out for animal victims of the chop of the mowing blades. Pepper, The Big Fellow, Bear and the egg-makers all love to find a mouse or vole and swallow it whole or in bits. All of us scour the fresh cut grass for our chosen meaty morsels. The Shepherd is highly amused when a mouse or vole is discovered and the canines, felines and egg-makers race to see who will get to it first.

By late afternoon the next day, the first tedding, or spinning out of cut grasses, occurs to assist in the evaporation to make hay. The machine tosses mown vegetation over and about. Grass on the bottom of the cut nearest the ground is now tossed up and to the top. The next day's sun will continue to dry the moisture out of the grass, which turns it into hay. Tedding must be carried out for several days until the cut grass no longer feels cool to the touch but has turned warm and dry.

Next, the drying grass is raked up into windrows that allow more drying by letting wind blow through them in anticipation of baling. Later, the dried hay is scooped into a baler where it is packed tightly in a net and dumped in the field. Freshly made bales must be kept sitting in the fields to settle and to keep from over-heating. The Shepherd and I pray no rain will soak them. We pack our bales so tightly that they will shed light rainfall. Finally, our properly aged bales, like a good wine, I'm told, are brought into shelter to stay dry and be our livestock's winter fodder.

My favourite activity is to help bring in the hay. As each bale is stacked onto our round bale machine, I sprawl in the cool shade. As soon as the quad's motor is started, I leap onto The Shepherd's lap for our ride to the shed where the new hay bales will be stored. I love the feel of the cooling wind ruffling my fur. When we reach the shed, I jump off The Shepherd's lap and sit on a previously stored hay bale. I admire how The Shepherd reverses the quad and its trailer and backs into the shed to position a new bale and unload it. When she is ready to depart for the next bale, she calls to me and I walk, trot or meander over to the quad for another ride out to the fields for our next bale of hay.

As our work with hay bales can be very hot, I sometimes envy that, unlike myself, my flock of sheep gets shorn. They can feel a cooling summer breeze against their skin once their thick woolly fleece has been removed. Sometimes nature seems very difficult to tolerate as the season changes because I must wait for the natural summer shedding of my long silky fur before I'm cool enough to be comfortable. I am continually clothed with three layers, much like a human. My undermost dress is fine silken fur worn next to my skin – it has been likened to a soft layer of the finest downy silk underwear. This inner layer covers my whole body. My middle layer, or awn hair, is equivalent to The Shepherd's summer T-shirt and jeans, but this layer thickens into a comfortable woolly jumper for winter. Finally, my long coarse outer-guard hairs differ a lot from my inner two fine furred layers but they most ingeniously act as my rain-coat and draw water away from my inner layers of fur cloth-ing. Hence I'm easily able to walk through fields with The Shepherd even when the sky pours rain, lashes sleet or drops snowflakes, which just alight upon me. I give myself a good shake occasionally to rid myself of excess water and re-fluff my coat. I remain dry as an old bone and deliciously warm under my three coats as long as a strong wind or human hands do not blow or flick my coat hairs upwards in the wrong direction and let in icy wind and wet to chill me.

Our handsome black Zwartbles sheep have a similar system of layered clothing, except the names are different. Zwartbles have short hair on their face and legs, this is simply called hair. They also have a small amount of kemp hair. This is their middle layer which can be short and brittle. It is also a medulla fibre which has a hollow or partially hollow core. Then they have an outer layer of true wool. Sheep shed kemp hair, as do most animals, after cold winter winds have subsided. While the middle medullated hairs resemble those that might become usable wool, these fibres lack elasticity and crimp, both vital ingredients for wool. Useful outer wool fibres must have the qualities that may be converted into felt or spun into yarn or threads that can be woven into cloth as warm wear for humans. This last important fibre is otherwise known as workable wool, one of the most ancient renewable fibres with which humans have clothed themselves for thousands of years. Before humans learned how to use sheep wool, they wore richly furred winter animal skins to keep themselves warm, the same furry animals they hunted and killed for food.

A renewable fibre wool is markedly different from human hair, or cat fur for that matter, because it has both crimp and elasticity. A high number of crimps, the crinkle in wool fibres, per inch – such as twenty-five – makes it easier for The Shepherd and the woollen mill workers to spin raw, carefully cleaned, shorn wool into a fine stretchable yarn. The elasticity of wool makes it supple and pliable with spring that permits it to resume its natural shape after stretching or compression. Wool does not snap or break into pieces like stressed hair or fur.

Interestingly, sheep wool is naturally fire retardant. How is that, you ask? Well, wool burns at a higher temperature than cotton because it needs more oxygen and when burnt, it forms a char that makes the flame extinguish itself. That's why sheep's wool is used in fire-retardant materials that carpet places like aircraft and trains.

There is another important way it differs from my fur or from human hair. Sheepskin naturally produces lanolin, a fine, soothing water-resistant oil. Lanolin oil naturally protects sheep wool and skin from the detrimental effects of wet weather and rough environments. 'Tis also important for the skin hygiene of humans, so much so that when shorn wool is washed before it is spun, the lanolin oil is saved and then processed into creams to soothe and protect human skin.

Wool is the only natural fibre that can absorb up to 30 per cent of its weight in water. When exposure to wet occurs, a chemical reaction in wool fibres produces heat. The Shepherd experienced wet-wool natural heating first-hand a few times, but most notably a few years after she had returned to the family farm in Ireland. In March rains, the River Nore often rises high enough to break over its banks and flood our riverside fields. The Nore, known as one of the Three Sisters, along with the Barrow and the Suir, rises in the Devil's Bit, before flowing all the way to Waterford, through a valley known as the Valley of Death because of the large number of ancient burial sites that can be found there. It flows past our three fields, named 'inches' from the Irish word *inish*. The Upper Inch is the furthest up river and the Middle and Short Inches the next down river. The Short Inch's name reflects its history because its upper section was a small field that was named the Well Field since it had many springs that percolated up through its soil. 'Twas sold long ago by The Shepherd's grandfather, who needed money for vital repairs to the farm.

One March day, The Shepherd and her father had a rush of blood to the head and decided to canoe down the River Nore from below the house down to Inistioge, a distance of some seventeen kilometres. The countryside is lovely, with a mix of willow, oak, ash, beech trees, grass fields, gardens, castle ruins and tumbling-down old mills all along her banks. The river is filled with crayfish, trout, eel, while seasonal salmon and the extraordinary-looking lamprey come to spawn among the otters and kingfishers along her banks. The river is also home to the famous Nore River freshwater pearl mussel, the only one of its kind in the world.

Stopping off in the village of Thomastown to meet an old friend, a travel writer, for lunch, the pair set off again, but misjudged the old salmon trap downriver from Dangan Castle, well beyond the safety of the huge stone arches of Thomastown bridge, and took a cold early spring bath from their open-topped canoe. The Shepherd's father, who had been wearing fleeces under his rain-gear, quickly succumbed to the cold, but The Shepherd's woolly jumper soon began to feel strangely warm, due to the heating quality of the wool. Quite what both of them were doing on the river at this time of year is anybody's guess, but thankfully, they survived.

Historically, wool used to be a mainstay and dependable income for many sheep farmers around here, The Shepherd tells me when she's in reminiscing mood. There used to be woollen mills as well as flax- and flourmills all along the River Nore. There is a road that runs along the river just across from our farm that is called the 'Woollen Grange Road' and not too far down our road are the old buildings of what was once called The Merino Factory. Here, a pair of local landlords produced high-quality cloth from Merino wool. The Merino sheep came from a flock imported from Spain. Some of these very same Merino sheep were later

exported to Australia as part of the introduction of the
Merino sheep to that country, which are now great flocks
that produce fine white wool. Now there is only a flour mill
and all the woollen ones have long since closed, so our wool
must travel twenty miles to Graiguenamanagh for it to be
spun into yarn.

Despite The Shepherd's use of modern social media to sell
our sheep products, she still loves traditional agrarian products from the Olden Days when they were made to last for
generations. The Shepherd tells me, rather grandly, that
Philip Cushen of Cushendale Woollen Mills has been 'a vital
part of the evolution and organic growth of Black Sheep
Farm's wool products'. He is a highly skilled weaver, she says,
with an innate understanding of the naturally sustainable
fibre that is wool and the process it must go through, from a
sheep grazing in our small green fields to a finished woven
blanket of the highest quality that can be sold under the
Zwartbles Ireland label. She is prone to lecture then, telling
me that this art of great craftsmanship and the understanding of wool is greatly under-appreciated in these modern
days of overprocessed artificial fibres. I can imagine, but of
more importance to The Shepherd was the help Cushen gave
her in understanding Zwartbles sheep wool and what could
be done with it.

Of course, I will have to take her word for it, as I personally have never visited Philip's woollen mill on a tributary of

the River Barrow in the village of Graiguenamanagh, as the spinning mule might roll across my magnificent tail.

Since the 1890s, the mill has skilfully turned fleeces of raw wool into yarn. First, they are cleaned, then teased and followed by carding into a rolled-up sausage of roving. Next, they are rubbed out into thin webs of thread, and finally, the mill's huge antique spinning mules spin the threads into yarn. Most of their wool to yarn machinery is old – from early 1900s – so visitors can be transported back in time as wheels of the spinning mule trundle across the mills' wooden floors. Indeed, The Shepherd describes Philip moving up and down his spinning mule while it spins yarn. He talks of his spinning mule like it is human: 'She speaks to me,' he says. He listens to the machine as she rolls rhythmically back and forth. He watches for breaks in the thread as it is spun into yarn. If a thread breaks, he quickly reattaches one to the other with a quick roll of the woollen fibres between his fingers. As spindles fill he will stop the machine to replace filled spindles with empties in a practised rhythm that comes with long years of experience. Like Black Sheep Farm, these mills have been in his family for many generations and The Shepherd likes that.

Going back to my coat, of course I can shed my heavy hairy winter clothing to keep me cooler in oppressive summer heat. Yes, I need help grooming the fur that I've shed from

The Shepherd, but I can barely stand it when she pulls at a matted tangle or snags in my knotted hair.

Unlike me, our black sheep are unable to shed their thick winter coats that derive from centuries of selective breeding by humans to improve their lustrous renewable fibre. So as weather warms in spring and summer, sheep lanolin runs smooth and thin in the heat of the day. The Shepherd rattles her Magic Bucket of sheep nuts and the sheep answer her call and trot in from the fields for shearing. Spinners and felters come from all over the Irish countryside to choose their favourite sheep and watch it being shorn. They ensure that they will have a lovely rich fleece to take home and spin into yarn.

Early summer often evokes The Shepherd's memories of her childhood trips to Black Sheep Farm with her older sister. She frequently tells the story of how her parents sent the sisters to Ireland from their home in the USA. Children were much less expensive to buy tickets for in those days. At age five she and her eight-year-old sister boarded an Aer Lingus plane at New York's Kennedy International Airport. Their mother was reassured by the cardboard dog tags with their names on them that were strung around their necks. They were looked after by Winnie Hayes and her team of friendly cabin crew.

To pass time during the flight to Shannon Airport, a very young Shepherd tried to make butter in the tiny containers of half cream, half milk that passengers were given for their tea or coffee. Neither her sister nor the cabin crew did anything to discourage her, so she happily whipped half and half for most of the trip. With no success, I might add.

The plane flew across the Atlantic to land in Shannon, where the girls were met by their granny and grandpa, who took them home to their Kilkenny farm that many years later would become Black Sheep Farm under The Shepherd's care.

One time, her grandparents asked a group of nuns returning to the USA to keep an eye on the young sisters. Clad head to toe in their traditional long black and white habits like a huddled flock of penguins, the nuns took them under their wings for the flight to Kennedy Airport. For some reason the flight was cancelled, so The Shepherd and her sister had to spend the night with their flock of nuns, who fussed kindly over them. When the delayed flight took off the next morning, the nuns intently protective of their young charges didn't simply sprinkle the cabin with a little holy water: they soaked The Young Shepherd, her sister and their childhood colouring books. She finds this terribly amusing in retrospect but at the time she was quite cross as the holy water prevented her crayons from working in the wet colouring book.

I have to agree that childhood memories bring forth all kinds of feelings in humans and animals. I learned the hard way how a pond covered in green duckweed might carry the weight of a frog but definitely not that of a cat. It's still a natural law that experience is the thing you acquire just after you needed it!

The same sort of thing once happened to The Shepherd when she was a small child here on Black Sheep Farm. The Shepherd's parents and grandparents told all the children that they were not to come to the porch for tea that day as they had a very important visitor. So all seven children went to play in a field well away from the house around an old pond. The pond's edge has a cement rim and they were playing tag, running around its narrow edge, precariously balancing, when someone pushed The Shepherd into the pond. On top of the water floated a thick carpet cover of green duckweed. Under the duckweed hid a deep mushy stinky mud evolved from years of rotten leaves mixed with cow manure. Upset at becoming wet, stinky and covered head to toe in green duckweed, The Shepherd raced up to the house looking like a green wet smelly little monster. No one was happy to see her arrive at the porch, although they tried to hide their amusement.

'No, you are not going in the house! Go around to the yard and hose yourself off.'

As she walked away, she heard more amused laughter and knew it was at her expense. Only much later did she learn that the special guest was Graham Greene, a very famous writer. So The Shepherd met Mr Greene as a green smelly pond monster. I'm sure he was able to tell the tale with much more of an amusing twist than The Young Shepherd would have – of the time he visited a writer friend in rural Ireland when their intellectual conversation was interrupted by his host's skinny blonde granddaughter covered head to toe in unpleasantly aromatic green duckweed.

The Shepherd's childhood summer days were spent roaming fields or being put to work in the farm garden, where she picked fruit, vegetables and flowers to sell at their local country market or to greengrocers. The Shepherd also remembers driving the farm's donkey, named Ishbel, who was such a steady neddy. She pulled a cart whenever they made hay, spread manure in garden beds or picked pears and apples. When there was no farm work for Ishbel, The Shepherd, along with siblings and local friends, would take her on all sorts of driving adventures. If bread or milk were needed for the house, they would all climb into the donkey trap or cart and, pulled by Ishbel, walk or trot – depending on Ishbel's mood – down to the village. There they would pick up the messages and buy chocolate ices for themselves, which they paid for with their wages from picking raspberries and currants or uprooting ragweed.

Once in a while they drove to Simon Pearce's glass-blowing workshop just the other side of the village. That same

Simon Pearce left the village later and presently has a glass-blowing factory in White River Junction, Vermont, with an electric power house driven by the White River.

His Irish village factory had a pool table on its interior observation deck from which tourists could watch glass blowing. The Shepherd, her sister and little brother would leave Ishbel tied up outside the factory where tourists took photographs of the donkey and cart while the children played pool.

Once when they were headed home from the glass factory with the donkey and cart they had to stop at the village shop for bread and milk to bring back for tea. The Shepherd and her brother ran into the shop to get the messages. Their sister stood outside and held Ishbel at rest. While the two were in the shop, a car full of tourists stopped and asked her sister if they could climb into the cart while one of their party photographed them. The sister obliged and permitted them to clamber into the cart. At the last minute, one tourist said they wanted one of their group to pose holding the donkey's bridle without The Shepherd's sister. Again she allowed them to do this. After lots of photos had been taken and tourists had dismounted from the cart, the tourist holding Ishbel walked away without a word, leaving Ishbel free. Ishbel saw her opportunity, leapt away and galloped through the village and over the bridge. At this point The Shepherd and her brother came out of the shop to see their sister running after a donkey galloping over the bridge full tilt for home.

Luckily, back then there was very little automobile traffic so there was no accident.

Another exciting donkey event occurred when The Shepherd was training a young white donkey named Snowball to pull the small cart while a friend cycled alongside her. Snowball was suddenly spooked by something unknown. Clenching the bit between her teeth, she began to gallop uncontrollably along the road. She shied back and forth from one side of the road to the other until one of the cart's wheels went up the roadside bank and tipped cart, donkey and driver over. The Shepherd found herself pinned under the heavy wooden cart. Snowball was stuck lying on her side, still harnessed between the cart's shafts. The donkey panicked, kicked and struggled. The Shepherd could do nothing, so she shouted at her friend to sit on Snowball's head until help might by chance arrive. As soon as her friend sat on Snowball's head, she calmed down, stopped kicking about and struggling.

Luckily, they didn't have to wait long before a huge lorry arrived. The driver had to stop since the trapped donkey, upturned cart and pinned-down Shepherd occupied the full width of the narrow country road. He hopped down from the lorry's cab, helped the friend unhitch Snowball from the shafts of the cart and then lifted the cart so that The Shepherd was able to crawl out. The Shepherd was very fortunate to have only suffered a bruised slightly grazed hip and thigh. Snowball was completely unscathed without a scratch upon her.

Another favourite childhood expedition was to drive the donkey cart to Kells Priory, six miles away. Back then, Kells was an unrestored Augustinian monastery dating from early Norman times, a magnificent hidden rural archaeological Irish gem. Few except local people ever entered the large rectangular walled keep, with its lovely tall corner towers. Partly surrounded by large fields, Kells nestled in the King's River Valley just below Kells village's two beautiful limestone bridges. Sheep and cattle of local farmers grazed inside and outside the keep on its rich grass. The striking ruined fortification and collapsed chapels were vestiges of a time when raiders attacked and hindered the monks' religious and productive agricultural lives. In its three acres of fortified priory, the square stone towers provided the children with steps to climb up into them. In The Shepherd's youth, they loved to climb up all the towers to see the different vistas of the surrounding countryside. They also would scarper catlike along the high walls with that immortal fearlessness of human youth. Furthermore, its many nooks and crannies made great hiding places all through the lower ground-level monastery ruins, so it was a most wondrous location to play hide and seek or sardines. Many birthday picnics with games at Kells are stacked into the long-ago memories of family and friends.

The Shepherd firmly believes that these exciting occasions and many other strong childhood memories drew her back, many years later, to her family's small farm in the Nore Valley of County Kilkenny. Personally, I think that the return to the farm brought her life to a full circle after many years of work in New York, London and Southeast Asia and I strongly suspect she would agree with me.

5

Summer Visitors

Summer time, June and July in particular, mark the arrival of our many visitors to Black Sheep Farm, whom I tolerate, because, as The Shepherd has explained to me, they pay the bills. She says it nicely, of course – that they are part of the growing Black Sheep Farm community that she's built for many years on social media. She often tells me that she feels farming is like religion. There are many different kinds, each one of which people are passionate about; that passion is what keeps them going through the tough times. She is a firm believer in to each their own. She will listen and be interested but doesn't like an agenda or belief pushed upon her. For example, here in Ireland, as a small island nation, there are a huge number of different land-types, which entail different methods of farming the same crop, be that tillage or livestock. She is very passionate about farming and utterly

dedicated to it, but also understands that one of the challenges of running a modern farm is how to make money to
keep the show on the road, so to speak. It's not easy with just
fourteen grazing acres and a small flock of Zwartbles sheep.

Despite being old-fashioned in many ways, The Shepherd
decided to move with the times and start using social media
as an inexpensive way to sell our Zwartbles sheep without
paying for the traditional advertising space in papers and
magazines. Our initial social media followers were sheep
farmers and others with agrarian interests. After that, many
non-farmers began to take an interest, curious about agricultural life, then knitters started to ask about our sheep's wool
and if they could buy some yarn spun from our sheep fleeces.
Loyal Black Sheep Farm devotees, who were not knitters,
were enthralled and wanted something woollen and more
finished, so The Shepherd designed Zwartbles blankets for
humans. Then The Shepherd was asked by her social media
followers to open a page for me, because she had often written about me on the Zwartbles Ireland page and apparently
people found me intriguing – which, of course, I am. So
'twas then I started my Twitter account, which The Shepherd
attempts to help me update daily. Dependent on rural
broadband, of course … In fact, when she was interviewed
about me in an American agricultural magazine called
Modern Farmer, the journalist, Jesse Hirsch, declared that,
'In the few short months since Bodacious the cat got a Twit-

ter account, he accumulated the same number of followers it took his owner years to acquire.' I don't like to boast, but I enjoy it when she grumbles about this, and you can imagine how annoyed she was when someone told her that I should be given more publicity ... Since then I have been filmed for television stories and documentaries about wool and raising sheep for both wool and as food, all of which I endure, because if it helps The Shepherd to keep the farm going, I am prepared to do what I can.

As time passed, and yarn and blankets were bought and shipped worldwide, humans found that their felines loved the real wool of the Zwartbles' wool blankets so wanted smaller ones for their cat friends. So my cat blanket was designed and came into being. One of my Twitter followers even used one of them to seduce a feral cat into his house and it has now become a beloved member of his family, so I am quite pleased about this.

Then there is Smudge's story. Smudge was a weak lamb and had to use the Aga to recover from the cold, before becoming a bottle-fed lamb. At this time, a woman in Florida was enduring treatment from a second bout of breast cancer. She followed Smudge's progress online and stated that if she recovered, she was coming to Ireland to visit Smudge. A year later, she flew from warm Florida to visit a chilly Ireland laden with gifts. She spent a wonderful half hour chatting away with Smudge.

The Shepherd also started getting messages and emails from mothers who would write and tell her how much their child in hospital enjoyed the daily updates on farm life on Twitter, or from children who, when they visited their elderly parents in a nursing home or hospital, told her how the first questions asked were, 'What has happened on Zwartbles farm today?' This warmed The Shepherd's heart, because she knew what it was like to be very sick and how welcome any distraction was from what was wrong in one's own life.

The next step for many of my followers was to visit Black Sheep Farm, to meet myself and some of the more personable ewes and rams like Smudge. They would book a mutually convenient date well in advance to come visit Black Sheep Farm so that they would not interrupt important farm work. Many, understandably, would love to visit during lambing time, but that's when we have all exhausted ourselves with lack of sleep and so we have settled on summer as a popular time. Our tour groups now come from the international world of knitters, farmers, cooking students, or even tourists from as far away as Japan, Australia, New Zealand, USA and Canada. So from the gossamer web of the ether is spun the golden coin.

However, while I put up with these seasonal hordes, whether or not I condescend to meet them is another question altogether. I'm a very busy farm cat. For those visitors who come to visit the farm, The Shepherd gives them a little talk on the importance of body language when they approach our flock. No sudden movements, no jazz hands, no direct eye contact – that kind of thing. I've heard her lecture many times, so I use the opportunity to snooze in the sun, occasionally tolerating a visitor's interest. While Pepper walks among the visitors to greet everyone in a dignified way, Bear, in his unrepressed enthusiasm, tries hard not to jump up with youthful exuberance onto visitors' legs – 'Hello, Hello, I'm here! Hello, Hello, I'm here!' The Big Fellow is usually locked away because he would get overexcited by all the visitors and worry that his duty as farm and flock protector was under threat.

Bear will bounce from person to person with excitement, trying to greet everyone with equal enthusiasm. Bear's love of life is infectious as his whole body gets involved. The Shepherd has to remind him continuously not to jump up on people, but because of his short stature he feels the need to add height to himself by leaping up on human legs with his muddy paws. For which The Shepherd profusely apologises, especially on wet days. Bear is well aware of not jumping up on The Shepherd as he knows she doesn't like this, but he has learned other humans don't mind. He is no fool and knows a soft touch when he sees one. This exasperates The Shepherd, but this aspect of Bear's training is impossible to change as humans love him so much. His charm overwhelms mud on jeans.

Before The Shepherd takes visitors to the fields she asks them an intriguing question: 'What is your first language?'

Most visitors reply, 'English', but often enough they say Spanish, French, German or even Japanese.

The Shepherd politely corrects them: 'Our universal first language is Body Language.'

She then selects a visitor who seems to enjoy his/her own space and suddenly she walks right into that space, close and face-to-face. She invades their personal territory, so they retreat a step or two backwards. I have to be on guard. Once I stood behind someone who stepped back rapidly and nearly fell over me. They barely managed to stay upright as I made my rapid escape – fortunately for me their footwork was quick. I wasn't the least bit amused.

'That's an example of body language,' The Shepherd says, as she steps back and returns the personal space to the visitor. 'There are a few things I trust you will understand before we enter our field with our sheep. First, we humans are predators because our eyes face fully forward.' She looks directly into the eyes of several visitors while saying this. 'However, sheep are prey animals because their eyes are on each side of their heads, which provides the greatest sweeping view of approaching danger.'

She points a finger to her cheekbone and temple. Then she rotates her wrists so her fingers make a sweeping motion that shows a sheep's ability to view much more broadly to each side. That enables them to detect predators better. Quite clever, I have to say.

She continues, 'Secondly, the sheep read your body language with acute instinctive ability. They fully understand predators as individual ovines (that's the posh word for 'sheep') and together they form a flock of like-minded ovines. Sheep may act three ways, as individuals or as a flock, towards you humans or towards feline predators. They may first choose flight and dash away. Secondly, they may repress their fear and stand their ground. Lastly, they may remain curious and not move away. We may enhance their curiosity further, dictated by food, hence the shake of the "Magic Bucket" of sheep pellets.'

The Shepherd shakes the Magic Bucket, the sheep pellets rattle and several sheep close by hear the nuts rattle. Right away they 'baaa' their Pavlovian response, which elicits smiles and laughter from visitors. And a purrrrup from me.

'One hopes the rattle will stimulate the sheep's instinctive curiosity and overcome their flight-or-fight instinct. Try to move with the slow grace of a ballet dancer,' she says, smoothly uncurling her fingers and moving her hand gently through the air until she points her fingers like a ballerina's hand.

'You don't want to wave or make jazz hands or any sharp sudden erratic movement,' The Shepherd says, as she breaks the elegant curve of her arm and makes it angular, a motion and display that sheep view as harsh. 'This will unnerve the sheep and they may flee from you. If you walk purposefully towards a sheep and stare straight at it, that sheep will immediately move away from you.' She strides with a strong eye-to-eye gaze towards another visitor. Her attitude is almost aggressive, so the visitor instinctively takes a step back and then smiles in understanding. 'So, if you approach them with your body at an angle, sort of sideways and not looking at them directly rather than face-on, you arouse the sheep's curiosity rather than force a fly-away response.'

The Shepherd's head and body assume a nearly coy angle sideways towards her audience. 'Now, calmly put out your hand to those sheep on either side of you but not the one directly in front of you.' Again she stretches out her hand gently. At this point Pepper, the Einstein canine that he is, will often sniff one of her hands to acknowledge and confirm this friendly gesture. 'Sheep read your body and interpret what your body "says". It's a mutually understood language of body motion and posture. As humans, we often misinterpret this ancient style of communication, which we've lost through development of our tribal spoken tongues. So, if you appear tense, they will read how nervous your body is and they will definitely not want to interact with you. On the other hand, if you are fearful, they see, smell and read your anxiety as if you are speaking to them, and they will stand their ground.'

The Shepherd and visitors walk from the yard towards a field. I follow them at a safe distance. 'Try to relax so you offer yourself with graceful calm as if you are simply a friendly presence. Sheep will then accept you and come over for a head scratch or push forward for a nibble of sheep nuts that you may offer them in the palm of your hand.'

As visitors walk towards the field, they pause to take photographs while The Shepherd moves to the gate. She halts momentarily. 'Do you have your cameras ready?' she asks, just before she slowly swings the gate.

Opening the gate often works just as well as a shake of the Magic Bucket. The rusty-gate squeak echoes across the field. Heads lift as one from grazing. Each visitor, poised with a handful of food pellets, takes pictures or shoots film as the stampede of black sheep races towards them. In seconds, sheep charge from every direction to gather around the small crowd of strangers. Some sheep jump sideways when a person moves with sudden 'jazz' hands or does not slide slowly sideways with grace. A friendly melee ensues, with giggles, laughter and squeaks of delight – from humans, that is. The sheep jostle, push and barge among the crowd of human legs to nibble or snatch at handfuls of proffered treats.

The Shepherd has what some individuals with long experience of tending animals call 'The Touch'. I've observed this attribute quite often since our paths first crossed in that novelty toilet-seat shop in Kilkenny. The Shepherd has told many tales of her charismatic talent and seductive skills with animals who respect and obey her right away. Even though I feel she occasionally exaggerates her ability, I know from my heart that 'tis true.

One day a young human came to visit. After he had observed the ease with which The Shepherd interacted with all our cross-section of domestic animals, he was struck by her anticipation of their every move. He asked The Shepherd how she had acquired her ability to understand so well what an animal would do next. Was it an instinct she naturally had? She replied, 'I feel body language is our first instinctive language, which is universal, so it can be translated from species to species. What works for a donkey may work for a dog as well. Now, I will tell you how I think I acquired the ability to read an animal's thoughts and to anticipate what might happen next ...'

I tell you, she has so many yarns she could easily clothe the whole farm in a woven patchwork of tales.

She went on to explain that as a child in school she had several problems that prevented her fitting into the conventional pecking orders that flocks of children construct in their classrooms and playgrounds. First, The Shepherd has dyslexia, which led to insufferable embarrassment when she was asked to read aloud. The printed word to a dyslexic can become an unreadable assortment of angular scratchings on paper. Because for them letters and words appear different, as if parts of the written words and letters disappear each time the dyslexic person reads the same page even a second or third time. I can tell you it is very similar to the misunderstandings that occur after I leave messages for unwanted stray cats to read and to let them know they shouldn't stray onto my farm. I do this by leaving territorial markers as ground or tree scratchings, but also with the additional necessary information of sprayed smell or cheek-gland musk. If I didn't scatter the essence of my personal eau de cologne other cats wouldn't understand my stay-away message and keep out of here.

Secondly, The Shepherd was humiliated when she was made to stand at the classroom blackboard with a stick of white chalk clasped in her fingers. In front of the entire class whenever she was asked to deal with mathematical sums, her brain froze like a deer in headlights. (I, on the other hand, as I said earlier, have become a master at counting my flock of sheep my easy way: count legs and divide by four.)

Finally, The Shepherd had what seemed a bizarre accent to her schoolmates in Charlottesville, containing not a hint of their southern mellow Virginian drawl. She sounded like a strange bird among a flock of local magpies because she used words foreign to their vocabulary, including many Irish-English words: 'biscuit' for 'cookie', or 'lorry' for 'truck', or 'petrol' for 'gasoline', or 'sweet' instead of a piece of 'candy'.

So, like magpies whenever there is a stranger in their territory, they attacked relentlessly and teased, bullied and beat her. Worst of all, they shunned her to avoid assimilating her different ways of pronouncing words, as if they constituted a potentially contagious debilitating disease.

The Shepherd's nicknames varied dependent upon the Magpie Parliament's humour on any particular day. To escape the isolation and dominance of the pecking order she drew winged horses in book margins and worksheets. She dreamed of escape by flight mounted on the back of a magnificent Pegasus. So 'Flying Horse' became one nickname addressed to her in derogatory tones, a name which I personally wouldn't have thought so bad. Her other disparaging name was 'Dog Face', which I wouldn't have tolerated for a second.

For The Shepherd to survive the bullies and the teasing, she had to learn to avoid both as much of it as possible within the bounds of the school grounds. So, for her own self-protection she learned from necessity how to read her peers' body language to prevent unwanted confrontation. She watched them approach from a distance as they walked across the playground or down a school hallway or entered a classroom. She observed their frames of mind by how they carried their bodies or held their heads. Facial expressions also formed part of the body language key, as did what their eyes said. Some individuals wore false beatific smiles across their faces but their hardened glancing eyes showed their true unfriendly intentions and gave them away as dangerous individuals who wished her ill.

She never forgot her ability to read body language, even as she grew up and looked for the next challenges in life, some pursued, others not. Animals were always her great love and she focused on caring for them even if sometimes she forgot them for a little while. After she abandoned her dreams of becoming an actress in New York City and London, she found herself drawn again into the animal world and took a job in a small veterinary practice in North London. While she worked with the vet she delved for ways to fund her next adventure. As you know, she is passionate about horses, and at this time, she dreamed of riding a horse in the footsteps of Thomas Jefferson's adventurous explorers Meriwether Lewis and William Clark, the first Caucasians to cross North America. She longed to repeat adventurer Aimé Félix Tschiffely's ascent on horseback from Argentina through all three Americas to Washington, DC. The Shepherd was most inspired by Isabella Lucy Bird, the first lady of international travels, who walked or rode horses over the entire planet Earth except for the North and South Poles. Amazingly, she rode on her own through the American Rocky Mountains during the dangerous period when the white man was colonising the country. She was never touched or harmed by Native Americans and others as she was seen as an adventurous free spirit who was revered as somewhat sacred and so respected by all she met.

It may seem strange in our modern world since humans now can gather data online, but twenty years ago, the only way of collating wildlife and animal-husbandry techniques and veterinary procedures, she tells me, was to travel to far-off places in person. When she worked for the wildlife charity, she befriended many exotic animals. She loved Sumo, an orangutan who enjoyed her gifts of delicious mango leaves, which she passed through his enclosure bars and which he took with delicate tenderness and chewed contemplatively. At another Asian zoo, otters gathered to greet her whenever she appeared. But her favourite animal behaviour story is probably that of a pot-bellied pig, which she's told me a thousand times ...

At the North London veterinary practice, vets were often obliged to do some extraordinary procedures that one would never associate with a typical small practice in a large metropolis. They once brought in a specialist dentist to undertake tooth extractions for a lady's pet pot-bellied pig. We shall call the pig, for the sake of anonymity, Miss Prigg. Miss Prigg arrived in a shiny black London cab. She stepped out of the taxi smack into the middle of the road, waddled across with her back end swinging side to side, and stopped all traffic until she entered the surgery. When Miss Prigg's owner handed over the lead of Miss Prigg's harness to The

Shepherd, she asked if there was anything Miss Prigg didn't like. Her owner said only the thing Miss Prigg hated was the sound of a Hoover.

The most difficult part of the surgery that day was to get Miss Prigg up onto the surgery table. All went smoothly, the dentist was pleased and Miss Prigg emerged from her surgery in fine dental and physical shape. As the time for Miss Prigg's owner to take her home approached, the pig had not stirred from her deep after-operation sleep. She continued to deafen all in the surgery with her loud pig snores. Time became of the essence, as her black cab had been booked for a collection time to return home. Miss Prigg had to be alert enough to walk out across a busy London street, climb into the cab and then walk up to her front doorstep at home. The vet became nervous and panicky, aware that heavy Miss Prigg needed to walk off her anaesthetic before her return trip home. He nudged her, tried tempting her with delicious aromatic food, giving her healthy pats on the backside, shouting into her ears and pulling her legs to full stretch in the hope of waking her up. All to no avail: she didn't budge. She lay far too comfortably on her post-operation mat in a cosy corner of the surgery and felt no need to budge.

The Shepherd had been out of the surgery to run an errand. When she returned, only fifteen minutes remained before Miss Prigg's shiny black cab was due to arrive. As The Shepherd started to pull the Hoover out of the cupboard where it was stored, the panicking vet yelled at her, 'What are you doing? This is not the time to Hoover!! We need to get this pig up and walking about!!!!! NOW!!!! Put that bloody thing away!!!' The Shepherd, undeterred by her boss, continued to pull the Hoover out and plugged it into a socket. She brought it close to Miss Prigg, switched it on, then quickly switched it off again. Miss Prigg's snore turned into a sneezing squeal and she scrambled to her feet. She looked all around, completely mystified as to what had just happened. Her owner had not yet arrived, so the vet and nurse stood on either side of Miss Prigg and slowly walked her from the operating room of the surgery to the entrance. Whenever Miss Prigg paused or thought how nice it would be to lie down again, The Shepherd flicked on the Hoover behind her. Miss Prigg rapidly got over her first wobbliness after surgery to the tune of a buzzing Hoover. By the time they got her to the front reception room, the cab had arrived. As luck would have it, it drew up over the kerb right next to the surgery's front door. The Shepherd hid the Hoover from Miss Prigg's owner. Then owner, vet, nurse and The Shepherd all helped a hefty, fat, but no longer groggy Miss Prigg clamber into the taxi for her short ride home.

During the summer months on Black Sheep Farm we sometimes have an extensive dry spell. This dry weather is at first most welcome for shearing sheep and making hay, but once we've completed these jobs, we welcome the rains that alternate with sunshine. Our fields need rain to grow our mixed fodder of herbs and grasses, along with the sun to heighten sugar and protein content. If the drought lasts too long, it hinders fresh green growth in the pastures and the soil starts to split. That means I must walk with great care to avoid putting a paw into these deep earthen cracks.

Occasionally I catch up with The Shepherd while she walks a field, head cast down as she scans the soil and grass to see how they are doing under the pressure of no rain. One evening in July, during a spell of drought and after she had a few glasses of wine with her dinner, I surprised her singing a song she had composed. She sang it to the tune of George Gershwin's 'Summertime'. She called it 'Waiting for the Rain'.

Summertime and the shepherd's been real busy,
Green sweetness Shearin' done and the hay is drawn in.
Come on, sweet baby, we're just waitin' on rain
So come on, sweet rain, come blow in my way.
One of these clouds is gonna blow in rainin'
Then your green growth will unfurl and sweetness will
    climb
in grass sprouts climbs so high, ewes' milk increases so
    lambs thrive, thrive, thrive ...

I usually keep a bit of a distance or climb into a nearby tree to watch from a branch in cool, leafy sheltered shade as The Shepherd paces the fields with her semi-demented singing. Pepper will lie down in one shady spot only to watch, with The Big Fellow seated next to him as The Shepherd walks back and forth, while Bear, with youthful diligence, trots along behind her to keep her company, and our newest addition, tiny Inca, trips and rolls along, every hillock and mound of earth a mountain for her to climb.

The Shepherd's favourite evening task in late August is to cook summer squash or marrow. It's not a vegetable I fancy – too watery for me – but she loves marrow and ginger jam and is quite partial to stuffing a marrow with a spicy minced meat mixture, rather like a Bolognese sauce. A marrow is an overgrown courgette or zucchini, which most people throw onto a compost heap, thinking it a hard-skinned inedible vegetable. She, however, slices it in half, takes out the seeds then halves each again, before parboiling till the marrow is just soft. She puts these on a baking tray with her cooked mince stuffed in the hollows and into the oven for a half-hour bake. She pulls it out to sprinkle with a lovely white cheese. A deliciously meaty, cheesy smell fills the kitchen, but even though I look hopeful, there's no marrow meat for me. She tells me that the onions in the mince mixture are bad for me, even though I'm not sure I believe her. This stuffed marrow is served with a white sauce and fresh parsley on top. Her *pièce de résistance*, as she calls it, is her famous ratatouille, a mountain of fresh summer veg: aubergines, leeks, red onions, carrots, courgettes, peppers, even parsnips, sliced in chunks then layered with garden-fresh oregano, salt and pepper, dosed in olive oil and drizzled with her 'finest dark balsamic vinegar'. She then roasts this vegetable pyramid in the Aga. Who knew that vegetables could smell and taste so good?

The crowning glory of a Black Sheep Farm summer, though, is showing our fine Zwartbles sheep during the summer agricultural shows. If we decide to show our Black Sheep Farm ewes, rams or lambs at their very best, we actually have to begin to make our plans as early as December and January. First, she selects the most noble and elegant-looking sheep, one whose distinctive white blaze goes unbroken from their poll (right between the ears) down to their muzzle. They need to have at least two white socks on their hind legs that resemble American bobby socks. White socks can be on all four legs, but sock height is strictly limited up to, but not beyond, their knees or hocks. The last beauty requirement is a bold white tip of the tail, less than halfway up the undocked tail. Finally, there cannot be a single white hair in the dark fleece or on the ears or belly.

Once these white markings seem to be correct on the group of screened ewes and rams, The Shepherd has to spend ages carefully looking over those sheep who meet the criteria, checking scrupulously each point of conformation. For example, she examines their pasterns – the ankle area between fetlock and hoof. Are they straight but not too straight and definitely not sunken low? A nice long black back with well-sprung ribs and a slightly rounded rump above a strong wide pelvis is essential. This anatomy first ensures the easy birthing of lambs, and second, that there is adequate room for a wide udder to make nursing milk easily available to a suckling newborn lamb. The configuration of the jaws and head are particularly important. The teeth must bite firmly and fully onto their pad on the upper jaw. Teeth must not over- or under-shoot, because it makes a sheep's head look like a duck's bill.

Once The Shepherd has selected what she thinks are the best sheep, she then pairs them against each other to try and decide which is the better animal of the two. They will have been shorn in mid-winter to grow a fresh fleece that would show off their thick, springy true black fleece with a good crimp. The tips of fleece hair must not yet have become bleached by the sun so that the sheep appear at their most chic in the show ring. There are many tasks to finish over the final few weeks before a show: grooming, primping, preening, cleaning and hoof-manicuring.

Usually, The Shepherd is so busy with visitors to Black Sheep Farm that she is only able to choose one show in a summer. One year, she chose the Clonmel Agricultural Show in south County Tipperary, which presents the Zwartbles Sheep Irish National Championships. The week before she was due to attend the show those sheep she had selected were led onto a sheep-grooming stand. This device has a lever that, when pushed, helps raise the platform upon which the sheep stands high enough off the ground to a workable height for a human to stand to groom. There is a cradle which keeps their head in position while The Shepherd bathes, grooms and trims them from head to toe. She does this with hand-held shears and a teasing wire brush, much like the traditional tool used for carding shorn wool before it is spun into yarn. It may be hard to believe, but some sheep love this kind of attention. They fall asleep standing up. When their grooming turn is over and the stand is lowered to ground level, they sometimes need to be pushed off their preening platform! I can't stand being groomed by The Shepherd, let alone refined titivation.

Part of this spruce-up process involves using a carding tool to fluff and fill out the fleece and trim with shears into a nice, evenly conformed shape. Careful carding helps to enhance or hide different elements of the particular conformation of each sheep. The carding brush is an unusual vital ovine grooming tool. Like a hedgehog, it too has prickly spikes. Each spike is metal with a small bend at its tip. The bent tips catch the crimp of the fleece and tease it outwards, which adds length to the hairs and volume to whatever area of the body that The Shepherd thinks might need a touch of enhancement.

I often sprawl in a shady spot to watch these laborious proceedings while Ovenmitt enjoys taking part. Often The Shepherd sits on a battered old wooden kitchen chair as she cleans and trims legs, hooves and bellies. Then Ovenmitt will jump onto The Shepherd's back and stand on one of her shoulders to oversee the work. On one occasion he jumped from The Shepherd's shoulder onto Alfie the ram's back. He crouched there and begin to knead with clawed paws the ram's woolly back, a feline carding brush helping primp Alfie's wool.

Much to The Shepherd's great surprise, our ram Alfie won the Irish Zwartbles Ram National Championship at the Clonmel show on a hot day in July. She jokes that it was a non-hurling victory for a Kilkenny Zwartbles ram in enemy – Tipperary – territory. She was well pleased. Hurling is something of a religion in County Kilkenny, and as every Kilkenny person knows, the 'Cats' as the team are called, are the best. The Shepherd is never prouder than when flying the Kilkenny county flag at the farmhouse, its black and amber bold against the deep, green fields as another hurling season reaches its peak.

6
Lazy Days and Family Visits

August is that month of our farm's year when our house fills to overflowing with The Shepherd's family, who all live far away from Black Sheep farm: her brother comes with his wife and sister with her husband and all their children. I tend to make myself scarce as the human young can be frightfully tiresome, though I have come to tolerate the old-young. Ovenmitt is such a lazy playboy that he revels in all the attention. He rolls over on his back, getting pulled and poked by many tiny juvenile fingers.

By contrast to my good self, The Shepherd is devoted to her flock of human youngsters, whom she takes around the farm to help her with small jobs. I follow along at a watchful distance, but sometimes cannot resist becoming more involved when the quad is used or if the children are catching frogs. Baby frog inspections are great fun for all of us, although I do get told off when I chase them through the grass and bat at them to make them jump again and again with my sheathed claw paws. The human young love to see these tiny frogs cling to The Shepherd's finger by clutching with their tiny toes. Only a fraction bigger than The Shepherd's thumbnail, they have just left the pond of their birth where they began as spawn and then became all head-and-tail little black tadpoles darting about. Their black colour hides them from predators in their dark pond.

Next, they grow into miniature versions of their parent frogs. They change colour from black tadpole to the fresh green of newly sprouted grass. They have charming dabs of earthy brown on their wee wrinkly green faces and little brown dots sprinkled across their backs. Dark brown stripes cross their powerful back legs to complete the camouflage colours that protect them when in grass.

Miss Marley stays well above the fray in our kitchen. She is so athletic that she leaps gracefully four feet above our kitchen table to land on the top shelves of our tall kitchen cupboards. Then she steps elegantly into one of the lovely big Mosse pottery bowls that The Shepherd was given for helping to sell pottery seconds before I came to Black Sheep Farm. A seconds pot has a flaw of some sort, which means it cannot be sold at full retail price. Miss Marley likes to curl up to have a quiet nap there. The humans regularly use these big bowls as collector-targets for the corks they toss up when they open a bottle of wine. This newly arrived cork in her bowl awakens the slumbering Miss Marley. She stirs sleepily, shakes herself and immediately kicks a cork back at the humans from her bowl. The cork sails high above the kitchen table and then plonks down onto it, which gives the visitors a fright that usually ends in fits of relieved laughter. Sometimes Miss Marley snores loudly when curled up in her bowl. This distinctive feline rumble resonates along the ceiling and throughout our kitchen. First-time visitors wonder where that peculiar buzzing sound is coming from. If one of the humans at the table lobs a new cork into her bowl and it plops on top of her while she is out of sight and snoring deeply, she awakens to meow in protest. The tips of her ears followed by her head make a sleepy half-open-eyed appearance over the top edge of a bowl.

While I'm curled on The Shepherd's lap, I've overheard her tell visitors the tale of when she lived in a great big city as a young woman and slept on her own shelf. Yes, a shelf – over a doorway inside a Manhattan apartment. The New York bed doesn't sound nearly as comfortable as our own 'shelf' here in the Black Sheep Farm kitchen with its warm Aga air wafting up on cold winter days. Miss Marley or Ovenmitt can be found most days curled up in one of the big bowls on the top shelf.

When we are young, it seems we will put up with just about anything. 'Tis only as we grow older that we find we prefurrrrr our creature comforts. When The Shepherd puts me out for my night work, which occasionally displeases me if the weather is blowing cold and wet, I slink across the yard to make my bed in a pile of aromatic summer hay in the stables.

In August the very important job of preparing for our lambing cycle begins. The Shepherd and I go out to the fields several times a day, where we repaint the ram's 'brisket' or the front of his chest, covering it with a harmless kind of greasy coloured paint between his front legs so that The Shepherd can see which ewe our ram has covered by the coloured paint marks on her back. It shows that our ram has done his job and mated with her. The Shepherd can then estimate the date that ewe will lamb. The formula for when this will happen is 145 days, or five months minus five days from the first day that the coloured mark appears on the ewe's rear end. This permits The Shepherd to calculate when we should begin the late-night inspections of our pregnant ewes in the lambing shed. Lambing usually happens in January or early February these days and depends precisely on when the ewe was covered. Luckily for the ewes and The Shepherd, I am an excellent judge of lambing dates after all my years of practice.

All of this activity means that The Shepherd's mind often turns to what she rather grandly calls her 'farming apprenticeship'. It began with her life in agricultural college in Vermont and then veered off-course to the theatre and to life in London, before she came back to the place that had been there for her all along. It happens to so many of us, that the path we take in life is not straightforward. It doesn't go from A directly to B, but takes a winding, twisty route. So it was for The Shepherd and so it was for me, who only embraced my true nature as a farm cat after some years on the streets of Kilkenny city.

Farm life really began for The Shepherd when she was a toddler at her cousins' farm in Maryland. She often recounts the story of arriving at their farm after dark one night just before the harvest of the fodder maize. The Young Shepherd had brought along a school friend who had rarely been out in the countryside. As they drove up the two mile-long dark and dusty farm lane, The Young Shepherd anticipated the glass of homemade warm drinking custard that surely awaited them on the old chipped white enamelled kitchen table. But when they reached the last fork in the road before the turn into the old stone farmhouse they saw flashlights waving about. The Shepherd's father stopped the car and opened the window to ask what was wrong. The cousins' farm helper reported that the Angus cattle had broken out of their pasture and had galloped into the field of maize, which Americans call corn on the cob. Everyone left the car except The Shepherd's little brother and her mother.

After they stepped out of the car The Shepherd could see why the cattle might have escaped while summer heat lightning flashed and crackled in broad blankets across the sky. With only the lightning to illuminate their way, The Shepherd and her friend walked into the Front Field, so named because it extended from the front of the house for a square mile. The tall maize stalks rose well over their heads, as harvest time was just days away. In retrospect I'm sure The Shepherd felt sorry for her townie friend, who was terrified and holding onto The Shepherd's shirt as she trailed behind her along the rows of corn plants as flashes of sheet lightning lit their way. Simultaneously, they heard the black Angus cattle crashing about through the corn. Suddenly there was a loud crashing very close to them just as a blanket of lightning flashed, and a big black cow emerged from the corn only feet away. The cow's head turned towards them both. The Shepherd's friend screamed in fright. This noise sent the cow charging away from them with her tail held high in the air.

When everyone got to the far end of the large Front Field, they then began to call out loud in a calm manner, 'Move along, sucky sucky. Move along, sucky sucky.' At the far end of the Front Field the farm helper called, 'Sooooweeee, sucky sucky, sooooweeee,' in the hope that the cattle would come to him. No one could see anything except when a sheet of heat lightning flashed to reveal the field around them. They could hear the cattle just ahead of them rustling through the drying corn stalks and mooing in answer to the farm helper's calls. Her friend still clung to The Shepherd's shirt as they walked back across the Front Field to the cousin's house, both still a bit frightened after their sudden encounter at such close quarters to an equally terrified Black Angus cow. After such an exciting encounter, the homemade drinking custard went down a treat. Oh, how I wish I had been there for their after-adventure to partake in that elixir made from the farm's own raw milk and fresh eggs!

After high school in her late teens The Shepherd attended an agricultural-forestry college in Vermont. There she acquired and improved her abilities in its formal curriculum so that she could earn her living in the country life she had loved ever since childhood. Often her learning from the practical physical labour she undertook felt deeper and much more pleasant than studying books, which she had always found difficult. She enjoyed dragging newly cut long tree trunks from woodlands with horses. She loved horse-sledging through snow among the sugar maple trees in Vermont's early spring to collect sap-filled buckets to make maple syrup and sugar. In these beautiful wooded glades surrounded with leafless winter maple trees awakening to spring with sap flow, the only sounds heard were the clinks of harness chains and the creaks of leather as the horses plodded and swished through snow, pulling the sledge loaded with sap-filled barrels. Later, she helped make maple syrup and scrumptious maple sugar. This outdoor wintry work enhanced her ability to observe and comprehend animal behaviour so that she and the horses could improve their work together.

Book learning was far from dull, however. *Soil and Civilization* by Edward Hyams was a favourite read and strongly influenced her future agrarian career. Hyams, a twentieth-century social and political thinker, was a strong influence on the organic farm movement, with its emphasis on seasonality and on man learning to work with the environment without destroying it, to provide the food he needs. The Shepherd is still a fan of Hyams, even if, she tells me, she follows a sustainable method of farming, rather than a strictly organic one. She does not agree with genetic modification and does not use insecticides, but she will treat an ill animal with antibiotics when required.

Rachel Carson was another author who influenced The Shepherd with her seminal work, *Silent Spring*, which changed the way people thought about the environment with its passionate defence of the ecosystem and its warning about the use of pesticides. Carson was instrumental in the banning of the chemical DDT from agricultural use. A powerful insecticide, it had a terrible effect on wildlife – however, as The Shepherd points out to me, DDT could also have destroyed that pest, the malaria mosquito, and thus played a part in eradicating the disease. But as DDT was banned, malaria remains a threat. She wonders if humans haven't succumbed to a 'God complex' of sorts with their own chemical concoctions. She believes they try to control or beat nature at her own game. The problem is nature has been playing this chemical cocktail game for millions of years, while humans have only recently joined in. I am not sure what she means by this, because I am a cat, but The Shepherd has read more than I have, so I feel that she might know of what she speaks.

The Shepherd advanced her skills further in animal behaviour during the summer after she graduated from agricultural college. She moved to upstate New York from her Vermont college for her first official agrarian job; she broke and schooled Morgan horses to ride. Morgan horses were an early American breed similar to the Irish Connemara pony and the Irish draught horse that could be used to work the land. She had become a licensed car driver at the age of fifteen, as many rural Americans do. At her new job she also had to learn to drive an ancient Model T Ford pickup truck to do many of her tasks on the horse farm. It had a button on the floor that you pressed with your foot to start the engine, a very stiff old steering wheel, a creaky clutch pedal you had to ease carefully or you would stall the engine, and such tight springs that you felt every grain of sand nearly bump you out of the driver's seat. She found out later that her early acquaintance with antique machinery had boosted her future farming career. By contrast, when she had to support herself with farm jobs she finally realised that one cannot learn all the encyclopaedic knowledge of shepherding or farming at an agricultural college. Farming needs careful observation and meticulous practice – I know this very well, because I had to learn my jobs from Oscar. One cannot learn to be a farm cat other than by dwelling and working on a farm. Oscar was instrumental in my conversion to and acceptance of farm life. He instructed me first on how I should carefully observe The Shepherd's practical farm work, and secondly, how to be attentive to his personal techniques of mousing and ratting. Often The Shepherd had to interrupt our hunts very much to our annoyance because she obviously needed our help with the sheep. She had become skilful at animal husbandry and land management as much by observation and practice as by formal academic education.

When The Shepherd returned to Ireland after her summer stint of breaking in Morgan horses on the farm in upstate New York, she needed to find work to support herself. In early 1980s Ireland there was very little available paying work, so most of her peers had emigrated to other countries to find paid employment. During that first autumn at her Irish home, it was not easy to find a steady paying job, so she looked for and tried a variety of odd jobs. All had to be within walking or easy hitch-hiking distance from our farm.

She began her odd-job work by picking brewing hops at a neighbour's farm for a local Kilkenny brewery. It was not a job to undertake without strong gloves. She picked and sold apples from our farm's orchard, which had been planted in the 1940s by The Shepherd's grandfather. The garden vegetables, soft fruits and flowers were sold at nearby country markets and greengrocer shops. Summer over, she next became a beater at several local pheasant shoots. That autumnal and wintry job entailed beating bushes with a strong ash stick to flush forth pheasants from all sorts of undergrowth. The noise of beaten undergrowth pushed the birds to fly towards a line of men with guns so that they could shoot the birds as they took flight. This job came with a midday meal and if the day had been good, the beaters were given a brace of pheasants to take home to cook, enough for a few meals. The Shepherd's cousin's wife, a master chef of pheasant cookery, taught her the best home recipes.

Many years later, the Shepherd's skills at cooking game came to the fore when she was given a haunch of venison by one of her students when she taught photography in Kilkenny. He approached her in the manner of a secret agent, tapping her on the elbow as he opened his bag to let her peek at a large slab of dark red meat, which The Shepherd accepted with delight.

The Shepherd loves to soak a diced venison haunch for twenty-four hours in an inexpensive ruby brandy or red wine with whole shallots, fennel root, carrots, a bit of diced ginger, a good shake of allspice, rosemary, thyme, pepper, salt and a goodly amount of juniper berries. Once the venison has had its long soak, she adds in a chunk of butter just before she places it into the slow Aga oven to cook all day long. The house gradually fills with a wondrous aroma, which triggers a universal Pavlovian effect in all carnivore and omnivorous inhabitants. She serves this with a rice mixture of brown and wild rice, which adds an earthy nutty flavour to the dish.

Another odd job The Shepherd took on was the schooling of a large grey Connemara pony. Its owner had no saddle and nor did The Shepherd, so she had to ride the pony bareback over the countryside. At this time The Shepherd acquired a dog she called Max, whom she had rescued (as you can see, there's a pattern here, as she has a habit of rescuing strays). He was jet black with his ancestry a cross of Border Collie and black Labrador. Of medium size, his curly tail was like that of an Alaskan Husky. Max never left The Shepherd's side. If The Shepherd left the farmhouse without him, he would find an open window in the house, no matter how high up, and he'd jump out to follow her. He was an incredible jumper and such a great dog that he would follow The Shepherd even when she rode the pony on asphalt roads.

However, Max was a bit of a qualified scaredy-cat in dealing with any other dogs. So whenever they rode through the village or passed a farm with ferocious-sounding barking dogs, he would use The Shepherd's foot as a step to leap up and ride in front of The Shepherd on the pony's withers. He felt quite secure high up there, with The Shepherd's arms on either side balancing him in place as she held the pony's reins for control.

Once when The Shepherd went on a long ride with Max trailing after her, they came upon many cars parked at the roadside. People sat in the cars or stood outside and all looked off into the distance. Max had already leapt up into his riding position on the pony's withers, so he felt safe as they heard a lot of noise coming from the direction everyone was watching intently. The sounds came from the Kilkenny Hunt, Ireland's oldest county hunt, as horses and hounds trotted along the road. They approached fast on this crisp morning, steam rising from horses and hounds panting puffs of vapour. The pack was owned, hunted and cared for by Major Victor McCalmont of Mount Juliet. The pony became very excited and Max began to feel unnerved despite being held securely in his spot on the pony's withers. The road filled with trotting horses, their riders and the large pack of Kilkenny hounds. As this equine and canine mob came along the road towards them, The Shepherd tried to find a place to stand aside and found herself and pony wedged in the crowd next to a woman she knew well. 'Why don't you go on and join the hunt?' said her friend.

'I'm sure the Major would never allow me to hunt bare-back,' The Shepherd replied. Just then the Major himself trotted up on a very large horse and surrounded by his large pack of hounds. The Shepherd's friend, who knew the Major well, shouted out, 'Good morning, Major, would you mind if this young woman joined the hunt for the day?'

With a quick glance at The Shepherd, who was mounted on a scruffy grey pony and no saddle with a big black mutt sitting on her pony's withers, he curtly asked, 'Can she stay on?'

'Yes, she can,' replied the friend.

'Get rid of that dog and you can tag along,' he said as he rode off. After he'd trotted a few paces away, he looked back and shouted, 'Just don't expect anyone to stop and pick you up if you fall!'

The Shepherd hurriedly handed Max into the care of her friend so she could join in the hunt on the pony. It turned out to be one of the greatest rides of her life to follow the Kilkenny Hunt that day. Back then farmland still remained very old-fashioned, full of small fields and meadows enclosed by stone walls, thick hedges and big ditches and often divided by streams and rivers. These rural parts of the land-scape, some man-made and others natural, served as bound-aries to contain livestock and sheep. Farmers had not yet fenced off meadows and fields to keep livestock from drink-ing and wading into streams and rivers. Very few farmers had sheep wire or thin electric wire to fence off their fields. Rarely one might meet a strand of barbed wire across a stone wall or on the inside of a hedge, but generally fields had not yet been made into small grazing paddocks contained within a thin strand of electric fencing wire.

The Connemara pony that The Shepherd had been schooling for several months was a solid, game little fellow and testament to the hardiness of the famed Irish breed. He jumped well clear of any hedge, wall, ditch or fence that The Shepherd faced him with. He was an unsung country Pegasus, a pony who flew with wings. The most exciting episode occurred when The Shepherd and the Connemara had to swim across a body of water. Riding the wet pony suddenly became like clinging to the back of a squirming, slippery eel. The Shepherd squeezed her legs tight as he galloped after the swim and pursued the hunt with leaps over ditches and banks and big stone walls. Luckily for her, The Shepherd balanced well enough to stay on board until the pony's back dried out from the friction between the body of the pony and the strong legs of the rider.

As the day drew to a close, The Shepherd realised that she had ridden many miles from home, so she had a long way to go in the dusk before she could end their day and rest the pony and herself. As she rode past a friend's farm, she calculated that she had a six-mile hack ahead of her and the dusk was turning to darkness. She thought she might dismount and walk a while as her body felt like it had been split up the middle and all sorts of muscles ached from so much fast, furious riding. She was about to jump off the pony when a young girl on a bicycle peddled up to her.

'Are you Suzanna?' she asked.

'Yes, I am.'

'My da said to tell you to come back to our house as someone is going to give you a lift home.'

With a great sigh of relief at the proffered gift of a lift home, The Shepherd turned the Connemara off the road home. She followed the young bicycling girl up the lane towards her family's farm, only half a mile away. The girl showed her into a warm stable, where the tired pony could rest and recover. Although exhausted, The Shepherd grabbed a brush and a handful of fresh golden straw to rub him down. As a typical Connemara, after a hard day's work, he snorted with pleasure as his head plunged into a big bowl of feed next to a pail of fresh water and a pile of last summer's beautiful hay.

Mr Hughes, the father of the girl, was very pleased, and welcomed The Shepherd as she walked into the farmhouse. 'Here she is, here she is!'

A great shout of 'Hello! Well done, well ridden. That was quite a ride' arose from a room full of people who had ridden on the hunt or who had viewed The Shepherd and the Connemara riding in the hunt from the road.

'What will you have to drink?' Mr Hughes asked. The exhausted Shepherd could barely think, so she just said the first thing that popped into her head … 'A gin and tonic, please.' Mr Hughes then poured a tall glass with three-quarters gin and a splash of tonic. The Shepherd sat relaxed. She hadn't realised how thirsty she had become and downed her drink much too fast. Before she knew it, a second had been placed in her hand. By the time her automobile ride home was ready to depart, she could barely stand after the quantity of unintended drink she had taken.

The Shepherd no longer hunts because she feels too old. She no longer needs the adrenaline kick of a race across the countryside following the melodious sound of hounds in full cry. However, for many years afterwards, friends and hunting people remembered The Shepherd as someone who had ridden bareback with the Kilkenny Hounds. They recalled how she had not only kept up with the hounds but also stayed mounted, no matter how difficult the going. After that long hunting ride the owners of the Connemara heard about The Shepherd and the pony's endurance. They sold the pony on the strength of that day's achievement. Well, if someone can ride a pony and follow the hunt bareback, the pony has to be a very good one indeed.

*

The lambing season in Counties Wicklow and Carlow was The Shepherd's best earning gig she tells me, and where she learned the lessons that would stand her in such good stead when she became manager of Black Sheep Farm. She was fed and watered, but earned only £50 a month – a pittance, really. I do better with my endless supply of crunchy cat biscuits, mixed with the occasional – delicious – raw egg. Not owning a car, she couldn't go anywhere to spend her hard-earned cash. Because money was so tight, when she walked to the local pub, she chose the nights when one could sing for a drink.

The first farmhouse in which she worked had flagstones that covered the entire ground floor. Everyone had a set of wooden clogs they put on to insulate their feet from the cold stones after removing their muddy outdoor boots. The Shepherd was encouraged to ride a small horse that belonged to the farmer's children, which she rode bareback around the fields to inspect the turned-out ewes with new lambs. This farmer had such a large flock of sheep and so much land that he had employed a permanent shepherd, a farm manager and several other farmhands full-time.

One day, after The Shepherd had been on the farm for four weeks, a herd of cattle needed to be moved to a new field. To reach this new field the stock had to be walked between unfenced woodland and a large field of unfenced winter wheat. All hands were called to help keep the cattle on the track and not permit them to stray into the woods or graze the young crop of wheat. The plan was for the tractor and trailer to lead the herd with cattle feed while the men and The Shepherd were to follow and flank the cattle. The farm shepherd, Noel, who had worked with The Young Shepherd for a month, suggested that she ride the horse to help herd the cattle. As they set out across the farm, the men all walked in a group while The Shepherd rode behind them. Noel walked in their midst. They chatted away together, laughed and slapped hands. The Shepherd sensed something was about to happen but she didn't know what that might be. When they moved the cattle onto the farm track behind the tractor and trailer, the men spread out widely to contain the stock. The Shepherd rode after the herd and watched to see if she would be needed to keep cattle from straying off the lane. As they approached the area where the unfenced woods were on one side and the unfenced young crop of winter wheat on the other, one of the road men who flanked the winter wheat side slipped, fell down the track's bank and spooked the cattle. They fled briskly away from him into the unfenced woods. The bareback-mounted Shepherd squeezed her horse's flanks, leaned forward and galloped into the woods to head off the cattle and herd them back onto the track. She galloped, weaving and dodging branches, trees and whippy young saplings, to get to the head of the herd. She gracefully turned the herd back towards the farm lane, where the men stood watching.

After that episode nothing more exciting occurred as they completed the walking of the cattle into their fresh fenced field. Then the men and Noel piled onto the tractor's trailer. The Shepherd rode behind and they turned to go back to the farmyard. Noel seemed very happy and he appeared to be collecting money from all the men.

'What's going on?' The Shepherd asked.

'Sure didn't I bet the lot that you would stay on the horse? They bet agin you, even tried to get you off by spooking the cattle, so I bet more when you set off into the woods. I won a packet!!!'

'Maybe you should give me some of that cash as I stayed on for you for two bets,' remarked The Shepherd.

'Maybe I will and maybe I won't,' replied Noel.

Noel taught The Shepherd a great deal about looking after sheep, but it's true to say that The Shepherd is no stranger to sexism in the farming world. She has become quite an advocate for women farmers in this very male domain. In fact, like the explorer Isabella Bird, she has always sought work that some might have considered the preserve of men. She tells me that she once applied for a job to work in one of the clean-up crews, who were paid very high wages to go to the Middle East and clean up burning oil fields after the First Gulf War.

I am Bodacious. This is my regular work crew. From left to right: Pepper, Bear and the Big Fellow. I'm the Boss — no messing around!

My apprentice, Ovenmitt, learning the art of lamb footcare. But he's desperate to know when he can return to the warm kitchen for a snooze.

Miss Marley evaluates the
wool of a fresh fleece.

Introducing our newest recruit!
Inca the tiny Puddlemaker.

The Shepherd lazing about – sometimes I think I'm the only one who
does any real work around here, and I tell her so! © Julia Crampton

Now that's one strange-looking, long-necked sheep . . .
Oh, it must be the new alpaca.

Why did you close the gate
in our faces?

Keeping an eye on one of my
egg-makers.

All this work for what? I think I deserve my egg now and I know there are plenty in the egg bucket. Let me at 'em!

Sit . . . Stay . . . Purrrrrrfect cat control.

Counting sheep can bring on the snoozes!

Top shepherding tip: never be afraid to stand your ground and show them who's boss. Even if they're twice your size . . .

Stop fraternising with the employees.
You're undermining my authority!
© Susan Wilde

Soil testing must be done so I may
as well enjoy the job . . .

Sometimes you can't help but fight
with your co-workers. And yes, I have
a scratch on my nose, but you shoulda
seen the other guy!

Sometimes trying to teach a
horse manners is impossible.
I try, I tell you, I do try.

Feeding windfall apples
to my lambs.

I have been told I have
charismatic eyes, which
command with just
one look.

Bringing in the hay before the rain comes. It's all about teamwork and planning.

Ovenmitt loves babysitting delicate, newborn lambs as they dry and warm up in the Aga.

What you looking at? I'm just working on my book and no one gets to see my prose until I've finished, understand?

My sheep never know when I'm watching, but I'm watching, always watching and counting.

Pepper and I work well together. I'm always in the driver's seat, while Pepper is happy to sit behind on the quad's rear rack.

A moment of calm as I sit among bluebells and cow parsley under a flowering chestnut tree.

This became impossible for her as women would only be employed as cooks or laundry staff, and this was not something The Shepherd ever wished to do. She was never able to see why a woman shouldn't do the same job as well as a man.

Now, to live in Ireland as a woman farmer with a flock of sheep has taught The Shepherd that, even though her farming colleagues and neighbours are nothing but helpful and kind, only occasionally, will they roll their eyes at her. Often The Shepherd recounts the story of a male visitor who asked her if 'The Boss' was in, and how she quickly put him straight despite the strong, outdated current of misogyny that still flows through some of the Irish farming community. Much like how I, as a Shepherd Cat, strive for parity with my canine crew, The Shepherd seeks to be equal to men within the farming community.

In response to this anachronistic bias against agrarian women, The Shepherd recently helped to found a support group for female farmers called Women of the Land. They named their local chapter South-East Women in Farming Ireland, or SEWIF. When the group met to consider what a logo for their group should look like, The Shepherd proposed sheaves of grain draped in the shape of a woman's eyebrow. This logo reminds farmers, female or male, of Áine, the Irish goddess of grains, grasses and early agriculture.

The Shepherd has continued to encourage agrarian women to rise above and beyond the role of seeing themselves as 'just' the unpaid bookkeeper or 'just' the calf-feeder, or the one who 'just' stands in the gap to keep the flock or herd moving along a chosen path. Instead she has encouraged these enlightened women of the land to assume the honourable primary title of 'farmer'. They are not 'just' anything, they are farmers in their own right.

One day The Shepherd was asked to speak at a SEWIF meeting to help women in her community summon up the courage to assert their sense of pride as farmers. To inspire them, she spoke about the history and evolution of agriculture. She reminded them that long ago, their ancestors belonged to tribes that roamed across vast lands and hunted and gathered within the wilds of nature. The women with children gathered grains, fruits, nuts and roots. It struck The Shepherd that it may well have been these early females, who had made food gathering a useful art, who also developed skills in caring for animals. Women who were breast-feeding their own babies might well have shared their milk with animals – orphaned lambs or goats, for example – it is a common theme historically and was practised by many tribes in many countries. So, it makes sense, The Shepherd knows, that the suckled animals would happily have followed these women gatherers. After all, orphaned lambs today follow dog-like whoever feeds them a sup of milk. Much like my many fellow female felines, who have raised clutches of baby egg-makers or baby rabbits and hedgehogs.

It seems likely that as humans moved from place to place, more animals would have been kept, tended and harvested to support the tribe. Women would have continued to gather grains while males kept their responsibility of hunting and tribal protection. This division of labour would have enabled women to become shepherds to small herds or flocks of animals, which would have followed them for feeding. So began the dependence of animals upon these early female agrarians who, according to The Shepherd, domesticated their newly acquired livestock. And these shepherds would eventually have observed that where animals had left behind their manure, grass would grow richer, greener and sweeter. So why not drop some seeds of grain in soil near manure? They would return to find stronger bigger grains growing, thanks to the naturally laid-down fertiliser.

So, to become a 'farm-her' became ingrained in women's blood, part of their evolution, if you like. Whether or not they agreed with her, the women present at The Shepherd's talk found themselves greatly energised with confidence by their central role in agriculture, and confident that they could still take up the reins to run their own farms and agri-businesses. Women may only own 13 per cent of Irish farms (and this figure excludes jointly owned farms), but this proportion of female agrarians doesn't nearly reflect their considerable contribution to Irish farming. Also, many men have the farm and herd number in their names but work off-farm, while the women do the farm work and still don't call themselves farmers.

Sexism aside, her work with Noel taught The Shepherd a lot about caring for sheep. She learned to recognise the difference between a ewe about to lamb and a distressed ewe who had a problem lambing. One time, while she inspected ewes and lambs two fields away from the lambing sheds, she was riding bareback with one of the farm manager's daughters sitting in front of her. She heard a ewe call out in distress and right away, she brought the horse around the fields towards the huge sheep shed. She swung her leg over the horse's rump and leapt off, landing on the ground with great ease. She then reached up and lifted the girl down. She pulled the horse's reins over its head and told the young girl to hold the horse while she climbed over a gate into the shed. She discovered and tended to the ewe's difficult lambing, put the fresh-born lambs with their mother in a nursery pen and gave her hands a quick wash. Then she remounted and resumed riding in the fields within twenty minutes, with the farm manager's daughter again in front of her.

The girl asked, 'How did you know something was wrong?'

'I was listening,' said The Shepherd. 'After a while you get to know the different sounds and tones a sheep's baa makes. They sound one way when food is coming and differently when food is late. When a mother ewe calls her lamb and when sheep friends call each other from separate pens, they make distinctly different noises. If a ewe has trouble lambing, she makes her own clear sound of distress. These are ways that sheep use to speak to each other and to us. As shepherds, we must learn to understand the different calls. Just listen carefully and you will learn the different accents and tones and what they mean.'

Part III
AUTUMN

Part II

AUTUMN

7
Mackerel Skies

The changing of the seasons reminds me of the old phrase, 'Mackerel sky, mackerel sky. Never long wet and never long dry.' Mackerel skies tell us rain is on the wind. The other saying that The Shepherd often quotes is, 'Mackerel skies and mares' tails make tall ships wear small sails' – in other words, we'll be in for some windy weather, or so she says. She also tells me that in France, a mackerel sky is called a *ciel moutonné*, or 'fleecy sky', in Spain, a *cielo empedrado*, or 'cobbled sky'. In Germany it is known as *schäfchenwolken* – 'sheep clouds' – and in Italy they are *pecorelle* – 'little sheep'.

When one works on land or with livestock 'tis good to know what weather is to come. It prepares us for whatever job we should do next, like spreading lime to help the soil grow good grass, or to expect that rain will soften the earth to ease our jobs, such as digging hardened dry ground.

September also reminds The Shepherd, and therefore me, of a perennial – and inescapable – problem on our land: dogs that stray into sheep fields. Now, you might well think that I would say this just because I'm a cat, but The Shepherd would like me to explain why it's very serious. We have had several incidents of dogs killing sheep in our farming neighbourhood. A few years ago, in a two-mile circle around our farm, three flocks lost sheep, killed by 'sweet, harmless' pet dogs. Only one farmer was at hand when two dogs entered his field, where they killed some of his sheep. Luckily, he shot and killed both – an act which might strike you as cruel, but which sadly is absolutely necessary. And it's the agrarian law: livestock farmers in Ireland are legally permitted to kill any dog that comes into their fields and disturbs their animals.

It's not just the sheep that are killed who suffer. Those who escape the canine attacks become so traumatised by the attacks of their flock-mates that they abort lambs. They are never able to breed again. They lose their nerve and deteriorate into sheep that are difficult to manage, since they've been made permanently susceptible to the tiniest stress. Just like a dog that has attacked once, felt the excitement of its wolf heritage course through its body and will no doubt attack again, a sheep will revert to her instinct of being prey, a hunted animal. And, as The Shepherd has told me, although sheep have been selectively bred for centuries into a multitude of different shapes and sizes, and that universally, all sheep have been bred to become flocking animals, deep within their DNA they still retain their ancient trait of scattering rather than flocking when predators advance.

Once, The Shepherd witnessed this phenomenon when she was with her granny, visiting a group garden project not far from Black Sheep Farm. When they arrived there seemed to be utter chaos, with people and sheep running all around the garden. The sheep refused to flock and persistently scattered in all directions. It turns out that these gardeners had grown marijuana. When several sheep had escaped their field, they wandered into the garden, found the 'Mary Jane' particularly delicious and ate it all. It seems that sheep will return to their ancient non-flocking instinct when they feel a desire to get stoned on marijuana …

Not long ago a neighbouring farmer called into our yard to chat to The Shepherd. Because I lounged on a generous soft snatch of stray hay in the yard, I overheard his story. He had noticed dog owners who stood and watched their tiny rat of a Yorkshire Terrier run after a flock of his sheep. They laughed as their tiny dog wreaked havoc among heavily pregnant ewes.

When he asked them to call their dog because it was stressing his sheep, they simply laughed in his face: 'Sure, it's only a tiny Yorkie Terrier, what harm can it do?'

Matters quickly became heated. He told them, 'I'll be getting my shotgun and I'll shoot your dog unless you call it in and control it!!'

They sneered: 'We'll call the *gardaí* (police) if you do that.'

'Go ahead,' the sheep farmer replied. 'You will learn that it's my legal right to shoot any dog that simply trots among my sheep, let alone one like yours, who chases and perturbs them.'

He continued to report that this brief altercation became very heated. The obscene language used and the lack of understanding by the owners of the misbehaving Terrier enraged him. Sheep stress is unrelated to dog size. Sheep panic sets in so rapidly that they may squeeze the life out of each other when stampeded and packed tightly into a corner of a field. They pile upon each other as defence to save themselves.

I would be absolutely devastated if stray dogs got in and killed any of my flock. Back then, when the canine sheep killers terrorised and murdered our neighbours' flocks, we only had a very small flock of Zwartbles sheep. We had begun with just four black sheep, and while our flock grew slowly in number, we all knew each sheep by their breed-registered number and by a personal given name or nickname. I don't know how The Shepherd comes up with some of the names she gives to our sheep or horses but I do know *why*. As our flock of Zwartbles sheep are a registered rare breed they each have pedigree certificates, giving the names of their parents, grandparents and great-grandparents. Having this certificate prevents inbreeding or 'line breeding', which means sons breeding with mothers, or daughters breeding with fathers or grandfathers. On these pedigree certificates each sheep has a name that starts with a particular letter chosen by the Zwartbles Sheep Association for each year. For example, in 2018, all lambs born will get names beginning with the given letter 'F'.

However, this does not prevent The Shepherd giving each sheep a nickname due to a characteristic, flaw or positive attribute. Take Aggee, for example, who has her own story of how she got her name, which I will tell you later, when it's lambing time, so you'll have to wait. Her mother is not a Zwartbles sheep but a cross-breed, a mixture between a Texel ram and a Suffolk ewe. She is one of the last sheep from The Shepherd's original flock, a daughter from one of the first few Suffolk ewe lambs given to The Shepherd and which Oscar helped babysit under the heat lamps so long ago. The Suffolk ewe is called The Great White Yoke as she is a big white sheep and because she has a mind of her own, which sometimes does not exactly dovetail with what The Shepherd would like her to do. The flock will follow her rather than go where they are supposed to go. This makes The Shepherd curse a blue streak and when this happens The Big Fellow walks quickly and quietly away to lie down well out of her sight, with a guilty look on his face. He thinks he has done something wrong. Bear lies down wherever he is and will not budge unless the sheep are about to trample him. Pepper tries to get next to The Shepherd and lean against her leg to try and calm her fury at The Great White Yoke or gives a hard nudge with his nose into the back of The Shepherd's knee to distract her.

The Northern Screamer is another excellent example of a named sheep. She was bought by The Shepherd in Northern Ireland at an export sale when she was a hogget (a one-year-old sheep). She was a nice-looking sheep and had a pedigree or bloodline that was not in our flock, so she seemed the ideal purchase. When The Shepherd got her home to Black Sheep Farm she discovered that there was a downside. Whenever it was feeding time or if food was late to the trough, this sheep would utter a kind of three-toned 'baaaa', which ended in a high-pitched scream till the buckets were emptied into the trough and she could inhale as much food as was possible.

Also, there is Pippi Longstocking, called Pippi for short and so named because she has two long white back-leg stockings. She was born in a 'W' letter year so her real name is Whippoorwill, after an American songbird. She is a great poser and has done lots of modelling for The Shepherd with blankets and yarn. When visitors come, they like to meet her, and can easily spot her with her knee-length stockings.

All this means is that we know our sheep by name and by personality, which makes it all the more difficult when something happens to them. So, when we heard about local sheep being killed and the neighbouring farmer's story about dogs worrying his sheep, The Shepherd decided to take matters into her own hands.

She wondered how she might better protect our flock and set herself to learning about it. She found out that there are four ways we can protect our sheep without our presence day and night in the fields. One is to find a breed of dog that lives among the sheep as a full-time flock member to protect them from intruding animals or humans that might be perceived as predators. These dogs differ from better-known traditional shepherding dogs, such as the Kelpie, Huntaway and Border Collie. The sheep-protector breeds include the Pyrenean Mountain Dog, the Komondor or Hungarian Sheepdog, with its distinctive mop-like hair to keep off the cold, and the big, white Italian Maremma ... They mostly work in areas where sheep-flock predators are bears, wolves, mountain lions and coyotes. These canine protector breeds are too expensive and too difficult to bring into Ireland.

The Shepherd then learned that a pair of South American llamas might possibly do the job. They are members of the camelid or camel family from the Andes Mountains, are rather large and have a nasty habit of spitting at their keepers. The third protector group are alpacas, also from

South America. They are befriendable, more manageable, smaller than llamas and gentler camelids, who come from the highest Andes of Peru and are fine sheep-flock protectors. They are quick kickers, whose sharp hooves lash out with absolutely no warning and with fatal results for predator foxes or stray dogs. Moreover, their fleece is gorgeously soft and warm. The fourth kind of helpers are donkeys, who are very protective and known to kill foxes or dogs by breaking their backs with a well-aimed stabbing action of their front hooves.

The Shepherd decided alpacas would be best for the Zwartbles, so she got in touch with Hushabye Farm in the foothills of the beautiful Slieve Bloom Mountains of County Offaly. This lovely place breeds alpacas with great success. The Shepherd travelled to the centre of Ireland to view the alpacas and see if there were suitable ones. Alpacas come in a large variety of colours, but she thought black ones would look best among our flock of black sheep. Also, she thought that alpaca fleece is such a beautiful soft fibre that it would blend nicely with Zwartbles yarn, both in texture and colour.

While at this beautiful small farm, The Shepherd found two handsome black male alpacas that she said she would like to take home to our farm. The Hushabye farmer and his daughter asked if they could keep them for a little longer to start them off on their halter training before they moved to their new home with us. The Hushabye farmer's daughter was very young but she proved to be a firm but gentle alpaca trainer for such a young person. When they arrived at Black Sheep Farm, she haltered the alpaca boys with head collars by herself before she unloaded and led them down the trailer ramp. Once the alpacas were housed in stables with fresh hay, clean water and a few sheep nuts to munch, Hushabye's daughter gave our two new boys a fond farewell with a good-bye hug for each.

When they first arrived The Shepherd kept the alpacas stabled for ten days so they could easily settle in. Stabling also made it simpler for her to catch them to practise sliding on head collars. They soon settled right in and began to chew hay and crunch sheep nuts, all good signs that their new home might not be a bad place to stay. Alpacas are very inquisitive but timid when they first meet you. They consider strangers as curious, possibly unpleasant beings. As a species they are very head-shy and hate their heads being touched. To acclimatise them to human touch, one softly strokes them behind the ears, down their necks and along their backs.

The first step for The Shepherd and alpacas to become familiar with each other was to feed them twice a day. She brought sheep pellets, which they chewed thoughtfully and indeed acquired such fondness for them that they began to search for them whenever The Shepherd entered the stables. So, clever human that she is, she lengthened the interval between entering and dumping food in their buckets. She offered a handful of nuts to each to convince them to eat from her hand and get used to human touch. They soon nuzzled her hands with their soft muzzles to consume the sheep-nut offering.

Next, The Shepherd continued the Hushabye-style of alpaca training twice daily by slipping on head collars for short leading sessions. She gradually reduced the number of sessions to only one long walk daily. With her gentle skill at persuading animals to behave well and to accept constraints like head collars and harnesses, she taught the alpacas in short sessions that became longer and longer. They quickly became used to her and to their new surroundings.

Taking time to train the newly arrived alpacas before turning them out into the fields with sheep would greatly ease the future handling of the combined flock of sheep and alpacas. Enabling a simple separation of alpacas from the flock when the sheep required treatments was essential. Furthermore, if alpacas know and trust a human, they will accommodate handling for their own care, such as dosing, hoof care, tooth care and shearing of their fleece.

One day The Shepherd took the alpaca boys for a longer walk into a big field with a steep hill that rolled down to the narrow public road. As she made her way downhill, leading them past a huge oak tree towards the road, a tractor towing a large trailer loaded with giant rolled hay bales was passing by. The Shepherd saw that the driver was so distracted by our bizarre long-necked creatures that he lost control of the tractor and was about to crash into the stone wall on the margin of the road. He suddenly realised his impending disaster, overcorrected his steering and nearly drove into the ditch on the far side of the road. This made The Shepherd giggle for the rest of the day as she imagined what over-excited thoughts had raced through his head. She could imagine him telling his friends, 'Ye know that crazy black sheep lady up beyond? Well, she had some queer-looking yokes she was leading about today. I was in such a shock, I nearly levelled the ditch.'

This story also reminds The Shepherd of one of her neighbour's reactions to the new arrivals. She received a text one day, not long after the alpacas had started to venture outdoors:

'What have you been doing to your sheep?'

'What do you mean?' she texted in reply.

'Have you been stretching them on a rack? Their necks seem to have grown.'

It would seem that they were the talk of our neighbourhood!

Additional training was necessary to get the alpacas accustomed to other humans, which was easy as The Shepherd had many volunteers. Quite a few friends with children came to see these fascinating boys, with their long necks and big, batting eyelashes. Even though they seemed a bit unnerved at first, luckily for all, they handled the throngs very well.

The next phase of training began when The Shepherd brought the alpacas into a field to get them accustomed to sheep who had never seen such creatures before and the alpaca boys who had never seen a sheep. She didn't want to let the alpacas loose with my sheep too soon in case they gave a pregnant ewe a mighty kick. The alpaca kick is the main feature of their ability to protect sheep as well as to chase foxes or dogs away. Unlike a cow, horse or donkey, who signal with laid-back ears or a hunched back before they strike with a hoof, an alpaca never seems to warn when 'tis about to kick.

The oddity each species sensed about the other was very evident in their body language. When the alpacas first met the sheep, it seemed that their belief was: 'What and who are those short-necked yokes?' A Zwartbles ewe in shock thought: 'What in God's name are those long-necked black yokes? Hey, Zwartbles ladies, come look at these funny looking yokes!!!' The alpaca boys worried right away: 'Psssst, I think we should clear out of here before we are surrounded by these short black stubbies!!!' At least, that's what I think they said. I now understand their language better but I did not then.

After a few visits the Zwartbles sheep finally got used to the visits from the alpaca boys: 'Well, those black yokes seem to ignore us and just hang around their hay.'

'Ooops, I think those black stubbies just got curious,' the alpacas said. 'Crumbs, I think they are following us now!!!! We better get outa here!!!'

At last the Zwartbles relaxed under the trees while the alpaca boys strolled by.

Then came the time to turn the alpaca boys out into the small paddock next to the horses' field. The horses and alpaca boys viewed each other with stunned surprise. Sensible Marco Polo simply stood still and took it all in while the mares galloped madly about. The mares circled around stationary Marco Polo on one side of the fence while the alpaca boys raced in circles inside the small paddock. The Shepherd left bundles of fresh hay for both groups of animals close to either side of the fence so that alpacas and horses would have to dine in each other's company. This separation by fence but enabling dining close to each other was a safety precaution until both species realised that they could live as friendly neighbours.

A few days later, The Shepherd brought all the sheep in. I sat on a convenient bale of hay to oversee the operation while she separated pregnant ewes from ewe lambs. We decided to let all the ewe lambs out into the small paddock so that the alpacas could meet some sheep on their own turf. Without The Shepherd standing between the two groups, the alpaca boys sought her out as security against the ewe lambs and stayed close beside her. She smiled at their insecurity and I could hear her say, 'Suck it up, boys. You are to become their protectors.'

Finally, we had to name the boys. I told The Shepherd: 'T'would be nice if their names came from their ancestral home of Peru and were of Incan origin.' We reflected a while, tossed ideas about and with Google's help, Inti and Punchau became their new names. Inti is the younger, blacker and more timid of the two boys and his Incan name means 'Sun God-Giver of Life'. Punchau, the older, bigger, bolder boy, is named after the Incan 'Warrior Sun God', whose weapon is the dart. So, we hoped our helper guardian protector boys, Inti and Punchau, would use their dart-like legs to kick any fox or stray dogs who might come into our fields to harass my Zwartbles sheep. (While the alpaca boys were getting used to my own canine crew, they belted Pepper with a kick none of us saw coming, so we knew what they were capable of.)

Last, but not least, came the day I properly met the alpaca boys. The Shepherd came into the yard with them one day after their training exercise, with both of them wearing head collars and walking on the leads. I greeted them and gave them the once-over: 'Right, lads, so you are our new flock protectors that all the fuss is about … Let's just make one thing clear from the start: I might be down here and your alpaca self is high up there with your long neck, but I'm the boss.'

If, reader, you don't believe me, I have photographic proof that this conversation took place. I was very firm. I stated my supervisory position on the farm at our first meeting and made clear that no liberties would be taken in the future by these newcomers. 'Seriously, lads, I'm the boss, so no messing about. This is The Shepherd Cat's rule on this farm!!'

After that, both alpacas lowered their heads down to my level and we had a nose-to-nose chat. 'There you go,' I said. 'You got the right idea. Bow down to a superior being!! The Shepherd Cat rules.'

8
Autumn Memories

Autumn sometimes reminds The Shepherd of her long-ago life in New York City in the 1980s. She'd left agricultural college behind and even though she'd loved it, part of her yearned to try something new, to test herself outside the bounds of her narrow life experience. Until she went to New York, she had mostly experienced life in the small city of Charlottesville, Virginia or on the land, whether as a child on Black Sheep Farm or on her cousin's Maryland farm. Later, as I've already mentioned, she trained other people's horses and had worked as a shepherd in Counties Wicklow and Carlow. Her student days had been ideal in Vermont and mixed in North Carolina, where she was shocked by the burning of a cross in a place still influenced by the racist Ku Klux Klan. Now, she decided, it was time to try to change her dream a little, and where better place to change a dream than in the Big Apple of New York City?

Of course, ambition and dreams are not like reality, and as she went to endless auditions, she was often told that she needed to lose weight if she hoped to get any jobs on TV soap operas. Soap opera, I would suppose, is a form of singing for soap. It must have been a dirty job as she never took one of those offered jobs. She managed to find work on a few TV advertisements; she had a brief small part on a TV show and acted in a few student films. In the city she slogged along pavements instead of through mud, which I would imagine would wear down the soul.

New York was an exciting place in which to be young but there was also great sadness. T'was the start of the AIDS epidemic, which destroyed so many human lives. Cat AIDS is quite nasty and I can only hope I never catch it. During that early New York AIDS explosion, The Shepherd had a number of friends who came down with this horrendous illness. People became frightened to touch anything anywhere. Some wore plastic gloves all the time. They carried their private boxes of gloves, wore surgical masks, drank from their own plastic straws and used their own knives and forks whenever and wherever they ate. Some dear friends died of this plague.

The Shepherd would know when someone was coming down with AIDS when they complained of a cold that would not go away. They would say, 'Don't hug me as you might catch my flu.' A number of friends had eruptions of red and purple blemishes on their faces which grew rapidly. Many people assumed it was a kind of skin cancer but suddenly those friends disappeared in silence or said they were going back to their home town and please not to call them. A great many wonderful, talented, creative, inspiring people were scythed down by this plague. The alienation of the dying was heart-wrenching. It resembled the long ago human Dark Ages when rat fleas induced 'Black' bubonic plagues that killed so many. When people continually feared for their lives, a modern version of the Spanish Inquisition of fear and bigotry descended on the New York world.

The Shepherd has many happy memories of New York City too. She danced in nightclubs with Sean Penn and Madonna when they were a couple. She hung out with the writer James Purdy, whose hands looked as if Egon Schiele had painted them. She dined with, went to plays with and spent time conversing with Tennessee Williams' last lover and secretary quite soon after Williams died. She spent time with Lou Reed as they had a mutual friend.

While she lived in New York City, The Shepherd had a variety of jobs as a waitress, bartender, model, actor, assistant director and stage manager to name but a few of the means by which she earned a livelihood. She stage-managed and assisted many different productions in

Off-Broadway theatres, located down dark alleys where one sometimes had to step around or over human bodies cavorting in carnal ways.

The Shepherd has vivid memories of the Westbeth Artists Community Theater in the West Village, where she worked for a time. The theatre was in a building renowned as the workplace of a famous inventor, Thomas Edison. He made all kinds of new contraptions that a cat like me really doesn't need, but one that humans depend heavily on was the electric light bulb. I never need light bulbs because I can see in the dark. As for the telephone that humans are addicted to, I don't need one either. I simply speak out when I need something and if no one is present, I just help myself. The Shepherd tells me that the first recorded message from Thomas Edison was: 'Mary had a little lamb', which still takes me by surprise. Whenever I hear my own voice played back to me on a video filmed by The Shepherd, I'm pleased by my work with the sheep. I understand and appreciate how effectively I explain what I do with and for our sheep to satisfy the curiosity of my social media followers. Incidentally, Edison also invented a new type of cement, which greatly improved the older mix. This kind of cement is what we use to repair our stone walls around our walled garden and our farm's fields.

The Shepherd remembers Westbeth with particular fondness, because the Irish curly-haired farmer I spoke of earlier visited her there one summer and she got him a job helping to build sets for a production she was working on. This favour would come full circle years later when he provided her with her very first lambs at Black Sheep Farm.

The Shepherd earned most of her income from her jobs at two small bar-restaurants in Manhattan's West Greenwich Village. The Cottonwood Cafe on the corner of Bleecker and Bank Streets served a Tex-Mex menu with beer and margaritas. Automatic Slims on Washington Street always played great blues music and served Cajun orientated food, delicious smoked mesquite grilled steaks and fresh vegetables. She enjoyed serving meals and tending bar there. Once, when farm-fresh corn on the cob arrived in Automatic Slims, The Shepherd stunned everyone by grabbing an ear of the flavoursome Silver Queen corn, shucking it, eating raw the kernels and letting the delicious sweet juices dribble down her chin. It's clear that she may have left the farm behind, but the farm hadn't left her.

Cottonwood and Automatic Slims were just a few streets away from the Meatpacking District, which was notorious for cheap ladies of the night and for black-leather-jacketed men's clubs, where they wore studded collars and chains under the Manhattan Highline. It was most certainly not a neighbourhood for a cat to walk about in.

I have been told by The Shepherd when I am feeling toooo hot during our occasional Irish heatwave that 'tis nothing like the claustrophobic oppressive humid heat of a New York

City summer. She often compares it to the heat in a rainforest, where, she tells me, a jungly afternoon rain shower provides temporary cooling. OK, OK, I gather one has to watch out for leeches in the rainforest's cool springs, streams or rivers, but the illusion of how to cool off is there.

Once The Shepherd described the blessing of a rainstorm's arrival in a particularly torrid spell in the city. She happened to be walking along one of the main avenues when suddenly the rainstorm pelted huge drops, nearly hissing as they splatted on the hot pavement, which began to steam. Other pedestrians fled beneath awnings or into shops to escape the torrential downpour. But instead of trying to escape the wet, The Shepherd revelled in the fresh cool earthy scent brought by the rain from whatever land its moisture had evaporated from. She ran and danced in the street and began to sing 'Singin' in the Rain', as a fine memory of Gene Kelly dancing in the cinematic Paris cloudburst. She saw that people smiled or laughed at her and cheered from their protected shelters from the rain. 'Come out, come out, enjoy this wonderful cooling wet manna from heaven!' she shouted. Several individuals joined her dance. They lifted their faces up into the deluge, sang the chorus to 'Singin' in the Rain' and enjoyed the cooling moment. Others said they would love to but hesitated because, 'I don't have a change of clothes', 'My boss would kill me if I came back soaking wet to the office'.

Recently, The Shepherd returned from a visit to New York City and to that apartment where she had lived on a shelf over the bathroom that I told you about earlier. She found Tina, her former roommate and an actress, still living there, thirty-five years later. They reminisced about those days and how New York City had completely changed. I find that reminiscence is merely superficial nostalgia. I prefer to focus on the present: when The Shepherd next might go out to make rounds on the sheep, stable, sheds or fields, where my next mouse is coming from, and most importantly, if The Shepherd is to give me a fresh, raw egg for breakfast. But hey ho – unlike us animals, humans love to time-travel in remembrances …

Tina and The Shepherd reminded each other of the mob hit just outside the front door of their apartment building and how, as they entered their apartment door, they heard a pop-pop-pop noise. When they looked outside after hearing the popping noise, they saw nothing unusual and thought it was just a car backfiring. The dead man wasn't discovered until the next morning. Rigor mortis had set in. Tina and The Shepherd watched from their sitting room window and saw the man's stiffened body being pulled from the car. The steering wheel had to be cut off to free him and it was packed with him into the body bag.

We know all about death and injury here on Black Sheep Farm. Whenever one of our animals dies in the night, we find them the next morning frozen stiff in whatever position death overtook them. The Shepherd usually tries to cover them with a builder's plastic sheet before crows and magpies fly down to peck at their bodies. The corvid family are notorious for plucking out the eyes of vulnerable sheep whether they are dead or alive. Sometimes when lambing outdoors, The Shepherd might find a ewe who is giving birth to twins. The first lamb is born fine and healthy and the ewe cleans and dries her firstborn. When her second lamb starts to demand her attention as it enters the ewe's birth canal, the ewe stays close by her firstborn but her attention is diverted and fixed on pushing out her second lamb. This is when corvids strike. Essentially on its own, the firstborn is a perfect target for eye-pecking. Any corvid will hop around the healthy lamb to seek their best angle to peck an eye or a piece of tender flesh. If I am nearby, I stroll across towards the bird, which often might not see me till the last second when I leap. If I am lucky and get quite close without another corvid cackling a warning call, I may take in a mouthful of feathers or make clawed contact with a black breast, but mostly I miss catching them. If I happen not to be there as a protector, The Shepherd may find a lamb with half a skinned tail, an eye missing or its poor back passage bloodied from corvid pecks.

It's a funny thing when The Shepherd talks about gunshots and that 'pop-pop' noise that they make. I'd really prefer not to think about it, but autumn on Black Sheep Farm, when the hunting season in November is in full swing, makes that very difficult. The only noise that truly frightens me is that from a fired shotgun. My pupils dilate to big black discs; I leap to the top shelf of the press in the kitchen where only Miss Marley and Ovenmitt go. I curl up in the farthest corner, waiting for it to be over.

My traumas took place many years ago when I first arrived in my new home as a gangly teenager. While out exploring our woods near the neighbours' fields, I heard people talking, then the shouts of canine names, followed by the rustling of lots of dogs in the undergrowth. They were coming closer, so I moved quickly out ahead of them towards the fields. There I saw lone men standing silently with what seemed to be sticks in their arms. They were at regular distances from each other in the grass, intently watching the sky above the woods. All of a sudden, the sticks came to life, cracking with bangs like thunder while pheasants fell from the sky over my head and landed with muffled thrumps on the ground all around me. I was stunned into immobility. Next, the huge dogs rushed all about me and gathered up the fallen pheasants, holding the birds softly in their jaws. I skedaddled so fast, I think I left half my coat behind on the brambles through which I dived to dodge a snuffling waggling canine, who looked happier than a pig on a hot day in cool mud. I left half my claws on the paving outside the scullery door when I raced around the corner into the kitchen, propelled into flight up the kitchen cupboard onto the safety of the top shelf.

The humans sitting at the kitchen table burst out laughing. 'Scaredy-cat baby Bodacious,' teased The Shepherd. 'Poor fellow, he must have met some of the Gundogs from the local shoot.'

They were half right, but what really got to me was the bang bang of the shotgun sticks and the pheasants, so like the egg-makers on the farm, falling to the ground with deadly thrumps all around me. I felt like Chicken Licken with the sky falling down on my head.

Ever since, I have had issues with guns. As soon as I hear them bang, I shoot up to that top shelf, which is otherwise much too hot for me with the heat rising from the Aga. Guns are my only phobia.

9

The Swallows Leave

The stillness of the moon belies the wind-singing branches and clouds flashing by. 'Tis nearly 3 a.m., but there's little sleep to be had as the wind dances through trees still heavy with leaf while their branches rattle across rooftops and rain thunders down, lashing at the window. The first of the autumn storms breaks the season into a rapid departure from summer.

My tail twitches as I contemplate distractions like my walk-across-the-yard adversaries, the swallows, who dip and dive at me to distract and drive me from where their young reside. But they will soon depart our farm with the end of their summer season. Before their departure they all gather to perch in rows chitter-chattering together on rooftops and electric and telephone cables. Why they don't just fly off, no one knows. It's almost as if they have to gather to share a leap of faith and to encourage each other to start their marathon journey of a migration. After they've gone south there will be no more lofty ethereal aerial acrobatics in pursuit of insects which live in our fields' grasses. During our long wintry months insect life nearly disappears, so swallows will have little or nothing to eat. My avian opponents will migrate to spend winter in sunny South Africa. We'll see our swallows again next year as soon as our Irish spring begins to glow.

About every two years, when September rolls around, The Shepherd and I take a very strange walk all over our grazing land. We walk through each of our fields in huge zigzag paths that look like lots of WWWs stuck together. It's time to sample our soil for its health. Is it too acid or too alkaline or is it just right? Will it continue to grow the finest qualities of grass and wild herbs to keep our Zwartbles sheep flock, alpaca guardians, horses and pony well nourished?

To determine the health of our fields' soil we have to begin to collect samples of earth with a most bizarre tool. It is a metal funnel but there is a crossbar welded across the wide end on which to step and push a boot onto. The Shepherd can press with her foot on the bar so the sharp narrow end of the funnel digs into the soil. To position the funnel and to carry it, she uses a long handle topped with a T-bar and she presses it three inches deep into the soil. As The Shepherd strides along she regularly interrupts her walk, plants the tool, steps on its crossbar and pushes the pointed tubular nose of the funnel into the earth. Her strong push makes a narrow three-inch sausage of sod pop up into the funnel's bowl.

As we walk in our crazy back-and-forth and up-and-down patterns across every field, the funnel bowl regularly fills with three-inch samples of our shallow rich topsoil. The top six inches of soil is vital to all life on earth. It is where everything grows, of course, which is first eaten by animals and then by humans along the food chain. If the sun shines brightly, I sometimes lounge in one spot and watch The Shepherd. Once she or we (that is if I'm not resting to contemplate higher thoughts in a nice warm place) have moved meticulously over a field, we empty all our samples into a plastic bag and label it with the field's name and that day's date. We do this in every field to ascertain the pH of the soil. The level of pH is a critically important measurement of the concentration of acidity, alkalinity or neutrality of soil. A balanced pH of the soil is needed so it stays neutral, halfway between acidic and alkaline, to grow the best grasses and herbs for our flock. If we find a field is acidic we might have to add lime to lessen its acidity. We can do that by pulling our spinning sprinkler behind the quad to spread granulated lime over each field. When we keep the soil at its peak neutrality, all the most essential vitamins and minerals enter the grasses and wild herbs through their roots, which makes them delicious for all our flock.

When the pH is in purrrrfect neutrality it also helps the soil to eat and digest the food we feed it, such as our well-rotted farmyard manure mixed with straw and wood chips from the sheep's winter bedding. These sheep-yard leavings enrich our soil by adding and keeping its micro-organisms, bacteria and fungi thriving so they contribute to the growth of lush, easily digestible rich herbs and grasses. The combined essential vitamins and minerals make palatable natural food. Our sheep stay healthier, their milk more ambrosial; it strengthens their wool and their manure becomes richer, which in turn helps continue to improve the soil to grow luscious ovine grass and wild herbs. The lambs grow faster and stronger because they enjoy what they eat. What's more, our happy sheep produce delicious meat. We tend the soil because Mother Earth needs feeding like any living being.

In early spring The Shepherd would have spread year-old, well-rotted wooden chips, straw and manure across those fields with the greatest need. In autumn I watch over these manure heaps, as they are so lovely to curl up on for a cosy snooze while warm steam rises around me into the increasingly cold air, a harbinger of soon-to-come wintry winds.

The Shepherd entertains me from time to time with tales of her student days in the agricultural and forestry college in the Northeast Kingdom of Vermont. Some of her most memorable adventures happened when icy air blew down from Arctic Canada and ambient temperatures of the Green Mountain State dropped as low as 30 degrees below zero. Added to the Vermont deep freeze was immeasurable wind chill. In this Arctic cold The Shepherd liked to clump through snow and ice to call upon one of the nearest neighbours of the college, an elderly woman with whom The Shepherd enjoyed chatting as she sat in her rocking chair on the front porch of her old weather-beaten wooden clapboard house. Despite the subzero winter weather, the ancient lady always offered her visitors a freshly frozen solid orange treat. The Shepherd always thanked her kindly but tactfully turned this generous offer down. Not bothered by refusals, this hardy Vermont woman just sat back and rocked in her chair while she bit with pleasure into a frozen orange, skin and all, which she savoured like a ripe apple. This wonderful rural peeress was a hardier dame than The Shepherd would ever claim to be or become. She lived beside a country road not far from Craftsbury Common, the village that was home to the agricultural-forestry/wildlife college. A friendly farmer delivered fresh milk in a tin bucket to her every other day, which soon froze on her porch. Whenever she needed milk for her coffee or for her porridge, she came out on her porch clasping a heavy metal spoon, thumped the iced milk to crack its top and scraped the milk chips off.

Luckily our weather in Ireland never settles to that low temperature range for any length of time despite our geography that puts Ireland in the same latitude as Labrador, a country renowned for its permanent frost. The Shepherd and I are grateful that Ireland is protected from such an icy climate by the Gulf Stream's rise from Mexico and the Caribbean Sea.

The Shepherd has many other fond memories of frigid Vermont winters advancing gradually into early spring. Snow still remained deep but the manure heap on the school's farm had enlarged thanks to winter's muck and straw bedding from the stables and barn. This high, very warm pile naturally brewed into fertiliser for the college fields. The students had to walk up a long narrow wooden ramp that stretched out over the pile, wobbling along as they pushed their heavy straw and manure-laden wheelbarrows. It tested one's strength and balance to dump them into the pile that steamed in the late-winter air. She fondly remembers social breaks after a hard day's work: late-night gatherings of chat, strummed banjos and guitars and folk songs sung before a blazing log fire on a giant stone hearth inside the students' log cabin. Sometimes they tired of indoor recreation and stepped outside for fresh air in the small hours of the morning. Then the group would walk down to the school farm just before dawn with the remnants of a bottle or two of wine and musical instruments. They continued to sing as they sat above the manure heap on its wooden ramp with their legs dangling down over the compost heap, its steam rising into the cold air. They would watch the sun rise over the snow-cloaked White Mountains to the east.

In another wintry adventure on a crisp clear evening, The Shepherd and a group of her classmates put on their home-made snowshoes and hiked through deep snow far into the woods till they came to a glade with a wonderful northwest view. They had brought a gallon of cheap wine and a box of matches and set about building a fire. They gathered the superficial paper-like dry birch bark from nearby paper birch trees, collected dry twigs and long dead branches from the woods surrounding the glade. As daylight faded their fire began to crackle and warm them. They removed their snow-shoes and stuck them by their long tail ends deep into the snow. Everyone sat on the extra collected log branches and quietly passed around a bottle of wine, chatting quietly as night fell while the fire strengthened and crackled. They all looked northwest and saw the spectacular aurora borealis ripple across the sky. I'm told that year the Northern Lights were spectacular all over the world due to Mount Saint Helen's volcanic eruption in southwest Washington State. The glossy, gritty volcanic dust had shot so high into the atmosphere that it amplified any colours of atmospheric relevance, rainbows, sunsets and the aurora borealis.

As the night drew on, the group decided to return to the college. They walked out of the woods and crossed a few fields. The Shepherd turned around and began to walk backwards awkwardly in her snowshoes to continue to watch the spectacular Northern Light display. She should have known better than to walk backwards across farmland. Suddenly and inevitably, she fell back into deep snow when she tripped over an electric fence wire that lay only a few inches above the deep snow. As she fell backwards the long tail ends of her snowshoes stabbed deep into the snow. Her body fell so deep that her feet were above her head and her legs lay across the wire fence – which was electrically live!!!! There she lay, helpless, stuck upside down at a most awkward angle with the electrical pulse regularly shocking her. Her classmates had walked further ahead, but turned at her shout. They became so weak with laughter at her expense that they could do nothing to help her.

Finally, three friends snowshoed next to her. They first cleverly pressed the empty glass wine bottle down on the electric wire fence, keeping it off her legs. The other two came beside her, reached down, grabbed a hand each and pulled her up and out of the snow. To say the least, she never tried to walk backwards again in snowshoes to look at Northern Lights, no matter how spectacular the display.

Back here on Black Sheep Farm, while I've been dictating this book to The Shepherd a blizzard is swirling outside as the Beast from the East clashes with Storm Emma, giving us unprecedented deep snow, so The Shepherd's practical experience in Vermont will no doubt come into use. So I needed no books for my learning. As I mentioned earlier, I followed my predecessor, Oscar, and served assiduously as his apprentice. I carefully observed The Shepherd go about her work. I moused and ratted to keep the stable and sheep-shed food clean. As I described earlier, I loved to hunt with Oscar. We stalked through fields, crouched low, sought brown rabbits and waited quietly and expectantly for that decisive moment to pounce. When he died in 2013, it was a very poignant deeply felt event for The Shepherd and pained us all. I still miss him every single day.

When Oscar died, The Shepherd had left our farm to take the ferry across the Irish Sea to attend the London Design Festival. The Crafts Council of Ireland had selected our very own Zwartbles Travel Blanket, designed by The Shepherd, as one of the items to represent Irish craft design at this prestigious event. She travelled to London to attend the first night, at which the Irish actor Stephen Rea would be the opening speaker. He loved our blankets and there is a photo of him holding one up to warm his cheek. The next day was The Shepherd's fiftieth birthday. She celebrated by returning to the Design Festival and exploring all the floors of the warehouse full of all kinds of modern designs for everything. That evening she went to the Old Vic theatre to see acting legends James Earl Jones and Vanessa Redgrave perform in

Much Ado About Nothing. After the performance she went backstage, met both actors and had lovely chats with them. It turned out that Vanessa Redgrave had worked with The Shepherd's great uncle, Tyrone Guthrie, as a very young, green actress.

The next day The Shepherd took the ferry home to Ireland. After the successful highs of London she was literally brought down with a big thump as soon as she landed back in Ireland and found that her car had been clamped. (The Dublin train leaves Rosslare docks half an hour before the ferry that crosses the Irish Sea from Wales is scheduled to arrive.) So The Shepherd phoned home to say she would be late since she had to wait for the clamper to come and unclamp her car and she had to pay a hefty fine for five hours of overtime parking.

Her father answered the phone only to tell her the very sad news of Oscar's death. He had seen Oscar that morning, curled up in loose hay on top of the bales in the stable. I knew Oscar had not been feeling well, so I had kept clear of him since no one wants overindulgent undue attention when one is feeling under the weather. In the early afternoon The Shepherd's father went out to see how Oscar was doing, only to find him sneezing up blood and shivering uncontrollably. He quickly and quietly sat down in the hay next to him and started gently stroking him. For a few moments Oscar's shivers stilled and his sneezes stopped. Her father then wrapped his hands around Oscar to pick him up and into his arms in order to bring him to the vet, and poor Oscar convulsed uncontrollably. While Oscar died, he was stroked, spoken to and held in warm arms.

As The Shepherd left Rosslare Port in her unclamped car, she drove towards home with a heavy heart. Soon she had to draw over on the roadside near the great statue of the Wexford Pikemen that commemorates the two centuries since the Wexford Irish Rebellion. She got out of the car, wept and walked around the circled bronzed men with their pikes raised high in tribute to history's fallen United Irishmen, the Croppy Boys and John Kelly of Killanne. She knew it would be unsafe if she tried to drive home with tears in her eyes, so she diverted her attention by walking around the statue singing a song she had learned as a child more than forty years before.

What's the news, what's the news oh, my bold
    Shelmalier
With your long-barrelled guns from the sea
Say what wind from the south brings a messenger here
With the hymn of the dawn for the free
Goodly news, goodly news do I bring youth of Forth
Goodly news shall you hear Bargy man
For the boys march at dawn from the south to the north
Led by Kelly the boy from Killanne ...

And poor Wexford stripped naked, hung high on a cross
With her heart pierced by traitors and slaves
Glory-o, glory-o to her brave sons who died
For the cause of long downtrodden man
Glory-o to Mount Leinster's own darling and pride
Dauntless Kelly the boy from Killanne.

I'm sure she used a bit of improvised dexterity to guess a few words as her memory might have lost some of the correct lyrics. There must have been a few passing motorists who thought there was a madwoman by the roadside, walking in circles around the statue and singing old Wexford rebellion songs, and her a Kilkenny woman to boot. They, of course, wouldn't have seen the tear-filled eyes. If they had, you can be sure someone would've been called to do something about it.

As you well know, bad things happen in threes ... When The Shepherd finally got home that day she walked around the farm to see how all the livestock were, as is her usual habit. When she walked into the horses' field, they all trotted over to say hello. She walked around them to check their legs and suddenly noticed a large wound on Ishka's right lower-back leg. It looked as if her lower leg had been skinned – her skin was rolled down her cannon bone and collected around her pastern and fetlock, the ankle area just above the hoof. She showed not a whisper of lameness nor discomfort.

The veterinarian was called to examine the leg and assess what should be done to aid healing such a wound. While they waited, The Shepherd started to clean the wound of all mud and dried blood. Ishka stood stone-still, not minding when her wound was scrubbed with a rough cloth to remove the stubborn mixture of mud and blood that adhered to the open wound. Meanwhile, I sat up on the stable window ledge well above any stray sprays of hose water or flicked soapsuds. The Shepherd cut Ishka's tail above the level of her wound and braided the rest of her tail to keep it out of harm's way. By the time the vet arrived the wound was completely cleaned.

He is a soft-spoken, kindly man: 'Oh dear, oh dear, that doesn't look good at all. That looks nasty, very nasty.' The vet explained how a wound in that location takes many months to heal as very little oxygenated blood can get into the lower leg. 'This kind of wound is called "degloving",' he said, 'as the skin is peeled back off the flesh of the leg like a glove.' The vet and The Shepherd bandaged the wounded leg. Then the vet made an appointment for Ishka at a specialist equine hospital on the Curragh in County Kildare – the home of horse racing and horse-breeding – to see what further treatment might be needed. It was thought the wound was caused when mares Mystic and Ishka were at play. Mystic was one of Silver's foals that The Shepherd broke in and trained and subsequently sold. At some point Mystic's hoof, shod with a heavy metal shoe, scraped Ishka's leg and peeled her skin down her cannon bone to her pastern. The long and the short of it was Ishka's wound took eight months to heal. The Shepherd became very adept at cutting away the proud flesh that appears when fleshy granulation tissue grows like rising dough around and over the skin surrounding a wound. Proud flesh is well supplied with blood, so it grows faster than the normal slow-healing skin surrounding the wound. This must be cut back so that the normal skin can begin to grow over the wound as a layer to protect the open wound and allow the healing process to complete. It has no nerves, so when sliced back, it bleeds a lot but the horse feels no pain.

One day while The Shepherd was cutting away proud flesh from Ishka's leg, a van pulled into the yard. The Shepherd had Ishka tied up outside the main yard but her blood from the proud flesh flowed down the slope around the corner into the main yard. Three lads rounded the corner when The Shepherd called out a welcoming hello. She was still busy cutting into Ishka's leg and blood poured over her hand as she spoke to them. She looked up just in time to see one of the lads being caught by his two friends as he nearly fainted at the sight of all the blood.

*

Due to the distraction of caring for Ishka's injury, The Shepherd got over Oscar's sudden death. However, I only discovered my lack of ability to hunt rabbits when I tried to hunt on my own without Oscar's innate skill. It took me many months of work but after one spring of practising on young rabbits, I finally got the hang of it. Ovenmitt sometimes comes out to pretend to help me. Of no use at all, he just sits, flicks his ears, twitches his tail and watches as I do all the work. Despite his inadequacy as a rabbit hunter, Ovenmitt does hunt very well when he chooses to seek rats, mice, voles and birds.

Once Oscar had died and his death had been mourned, I shouldered the mantle of top cat with ease. My authority was never questioned by any of the other resident felines or canines.

My status is particularly helpful when The Shepherd is preparing the many meals she cooks when there is a glut of good food, which, when cooked and frozen, will see us through the long, bitter winter. September is our month of many harvests, after all. We pick apples and pears, and a local man also collects apples from Black Sheep Farm to make into cider and apple brandy, which The Shepherd tells me is delicious. We dig potatoes and harvest the wether (castrated) lambs for eating.

The Shepherd makes delicious lamb stews with lovely lamb chops, fresh carrots, potatoes, apples and pears all cooked together. I watch for hours, giving pointers to her as to what garden herbs and spices she should add to these future culinary delights.

Huge pots of stew or chilli, shepherd's pies, soups or pasta sauces are produced and then frozen in portions for two people. That way if there is a sudden influx of visitors 'tis easy to produce a quick homemade meal. She thanks me with raw meaty bits or a raw egg. Our feline and canine work crew lines up several times a week for chopped morsels of raw liver and heart, which we all love and which are naturally rich in vitamins and minerals. These meat treats help us to grow our thick coats for the coming winter months.

We also have a most pleasant lip-smacking job to which we are all very diligently attentive, which is to pre-rinse pots, pans and plates before they're placed in the dishwasher. Sometimes a real treat comes along in the form of raw milk. Now, raw milk, unlike homogenised or pasteurised milk, is fine for felines as Dr Francis Pottenger's ten-year research into the diets of felines shows. He conducted his research way back in the 1930s and 40s, discovering that a diet of raw meat and milk produced far healthier cats than a diet of treated milk and cooked food – so don't let anyone tell you raw milk is bad for cats. It is the pasteurised and homogenised version that is harmful to our feline digestive tracts. I will say nothing about raw versus pasteurised milk for human consumption as our carnivore traits and tendencies differ and I firmly believe to each their own. Humans, being omnivores, can be picky and will choose a dietary preference to suit their own cultural, societal, philosophical and financial preference.

Part IV
WINTER

10
The Early-Winter Chills

Still air lets chimney smoke sail up ramrod-straight, no bends anywhere in its smoky grey trail of vapour. Stars glitter in clear black sky. Grass grows slowly now as autumnal nights lengthen and we await the first frost. Will winter be hard or will it be mild enough for grass to grow slowly through its dark months and perhaps permit the sheep to graze?

As autumn slips into winter, The Shepherd is reminded of long-ago season-markers when she lived in the Appalachian Mountains. She dwelt in a log cabin on a farm in the foothills of the Blue Ridge Mountains next to Shenandoah National Park. She recalled how after the first really frosty nights of autumn, scents of burning pig hair and rendered pig fat drifted up from the glen below her cabin. Local families butchered pigs they had fattened all summer till autumn, or fall as it is called in America. They had brought them down to icy spring-fed mountain streams. There they built fires beneath vats, burned off pigs' hair and rendered pig fat for cooking throughout the next year.

Another vivid memory that The Shepherd often shares with me was of riding her horse through fields of cattle she helped to look after. One day she startled a black bear stalking a cow which had just calved. Very likely the bear was only looking to feast on the afterbirth, but The Shepherd could not risk the bear remaining so near the newborn calf and mother cow. She squeezed her legs to urge her horse to gallop straight at the bear. At the top of her lungs she yelled to frighten it away. The bear fled across the field to escape the mounted demon, half horse, half woman, whose hoof beats thundered, speeding towards it, long hair flying, a female rendition of Chiron the Centaur or a Scythian warrior maiden. The speed of the fugitive bear was incredibly so much faster than the human anticipated. She had expected she would get close to the bear on a horse at full gallop, but instead, as the bear gathered speed, the frightened animal ran straight into a four-foot wire cattle fence. When The Shepherd grasped the terrified bear's predicament, she pulled the reins of her snorting horse and slowed down so the bear could resolve its panic and think how to escape. The bear sped along the wire fence, came to the corner of the field and leapt over and away with a magnificent jump. After landing safely on the far side, it splashed across the small stream that separated the cattle fields from its homeland and disappeared into the deep woods of Shenandoah National Park.

The only cattle wrangling The Shepherd does here in Ireland is when a neighbour needs help, which happened about a year ago. We were just walking across our farmyard to do some work when a stranger pulled up in a car and ran up to us. He had been for a walk in the fields on the far side of the river from our farm, when he saw a cow break clean through the electric fence that bordered the field and fall down the ten-foot bank into the water. He could see that it could not get out. Our farmhouse is visible up on the hill where it overlooks the river valley, so he had assumed the cow was one of ours. He called up to let us know, which was very neighbourly of him.

The Shepherd thought for a few minutes, figured out whose cow it was and called the owner. Then she jumped onto the quad and raced down to the road and crossed the field to the river. Sadly, she didn't let me go with her, so I had to rely on her report of the drama when she got home ...

When she got there, the cow was in deep water trying to keep afloat. The Shepherd tried to make her walk upriver to a shallow incline, but she would only go a few paces. The Shepherd told me there was heavy vegetation on the bank above the animal so she only managed to find a spot with no trees or shrubs, but the beast just couldn't manage to get out. The cow's owner turned up. He got into the river to try and help her walk upriver to an easy place in the bank to get out. But she was exhausted so The Shepherd called the vet and another neighbour, who had a JCB machine with a telescopic handler, somewhat like a forklift. The cow's owner, who was still in the river, managed to attach belts around the cow while the others on the bank attached the belts onto the fork prongs of the machine. They then lifted the huge, heavy animal out of the river.

Two vets attended the rescue operation in case anything went wrong or if the cow needed some veterinary attention. Six humans collected there to help rescue the cow, who was a bit shaken, but who recovered from her ordeal. The Shepherd loves how there is always a great willingness among farmer neighbours to help each other in times of need and at a moment's notice. They drop whatever they are doing and come quickly to help each other out.

Only moments after The Shepherd got back to our yard after the dramatic cow rescue, she got a phone call telling her more cattle from another neighbour had broken out of their field onto our busy main road. The Shepherd leapt onto our quad bike and buzzed off with Pepper riding shotgun behind her to herd the escaped cattle off the road. On other occasions, neighbours have helped The Shepherd to recover our sheep when they have escaped onto the public road below our farm, or have brought hay out to livestock when the quad broke down or during deep snow.

Pre-winter tasks include clearing drains, stacking firewood and preparing feed for our sheep. To do this, we have to collect our gigantic round hay bales that we store in The Shepherd's cousin's barn. His farm is next to Black Sheep Farm but we must still drive our bales one at a time along two miles of rough lanes from his barn to our sheep shed and stables. Come rain or shine, wind or snow, The Shepherd must cleverly wedge each single heavy bale to fit into her specially designed round bale trailer. Then she pulls the trailer home with our quad that is like our tractor, with Pepper, as usual, riding behind to keep her company. We deliver each bale to our hungry sheep directly into the grazing fields when there is little grass in good weather and undercover into the sheep feeding shed in rough winter weather.

One of her least favourite jobs at this time of year is mucking out. But the hard physical work reminds The Shepherd of just how far she's come since the illness that struck her down over twenty years ago. Whenever she mucks out a shed in spring that is full of sheep manure or lies on the wet ground in pouring rain or stretches flat upon the damp stable floor to reach in up to her elbow to unclog a blocked drain, she can recall how long she spent in bed with a fevered foggy brain and body racked with pain. Whenever she mucks out a stable she still feels her physical movement in every muscle. She can't help but remember how much she suffered and she has to wonder if her illness might return unexpectedly. She senses how each muscle carries its share of work to keep her legs upright, to move with fluid strength, to sift a sprong (a three tined fork) through straw, to pick up manure and to toss sprongfuls into the wheelbarrow. She wheels the heavy barrow that tests her combined muscle and mind power to reach the muck heap. The weighty load has to be pushed by its handles to the top of the pile, tipped to empty and wheeled back for the next load.

Every morning she wakes up in hope that her body will carry her through another day. Some days prove better than others, but even if truly bad days are now further apart, she is always haunted by the feeling that her body might suddenly surrender to her illness again.

With Pepper's assistance I also oversee The Shepherd continuously as caretaker and sometimes have to nurse her full-time. You see, Pepper ingeniously senses whenever The Shepherd's tropical fever is about to recur well before she does. Even though The Shepherd has learned over the years the kind of warning signals her body may give and what symptoms to keep an eye out for, it's Pepper who will lean firmly against her leg, sensing all is not well. He pushes so ridiculously close that he almost trips her if she stands or steps forward. He presses her leg to warn her to become aware that it is time for her to stop whatever she is doing and go straight to bed to rest. The sooner she goes to bed, the quicker she will recover to resume her duties on our farm. While she is in bed, I mind all our house and farm activities.

How and where does one begin to explain The Shepherd's sporadically debilitating illness, which I alluded to at the beginning of this book? After she returned to London from what became her last work project in Southeast Asia, she was suddenly overwhelmed by fever. She had loved her job and found it a perfect fit from which to make up her lack of postgraduate education. She helped care for extraordinary varieties of tropical animal species. She met fascinating people with interests similar to hers and had new entertaining adventures daily. She had deeply loved this work with wild exotic animals and the warm lovely people she met and worked with.

Exhausted by months of long hours in humid tropical heat, wildlife parks, zoos and rainforests, and many hours of travel, often by primitive means, she suddenly sensed something was profoundly amiss. She had walked into the Oxford Street Tube station to the top of the escalators that plunge down to the Underground. As the top moving step slowly brought her into the subterranean underworld, she felt herself spin. Her world became a revolving technicolor kaleidoscope. Fortunately, another human was standing a step below her, so she knew she could not fall down the flight of moving stairs. She hurried home to bed for what she thought was only exhaustion from jet lag and frenetic, difficult work. She thought that a good night's sleep would banish her malaise. Sadly, that was not to be, as a visit to the Royal Hospital for Tropical Diseases confirmed what she had initially thought might have been a simple flu or dose of toxoplasmosis was probably something more serious and difficult to treat.

As soon as The Shepherd lay down upon her hospital bed, she felt her body let itself go, as it had found a safe place to collapse. She had enormous muscular pain. She suffered pounding headaches that she described as feeling as if she had a watermelon-sized brain confined within a pea-sized skull. During her first week in hospital, she underwent a plethora of tests for tropical diseases. Some tests were revolting, like one called the string test, in which she had to swallow a pill the size of her pinky finger attached to a long length of coarse string. One end of the string hung out of her mouth. The nurse held one end of loose string while The Shepherd swallowed the huge pill and the long string. Once the pill and string had been swallowed, its loose end of string was taped to The Shepherd's cheek. Many hours passed with no food permitted to protect the string from stomach acid and digestive enzymes. The string and pill capsule passed almost all the way down through The Shepherd's small and large intestine. The nurse then pulled the string slowly back through The Shepherd's throat and she gagged with nausea as it slid from her throat and mouth. This kind of string test was one of the few ways to look for particular kinds of tropical parasites. However, one blood test confirmed that The Shepherd had, in fact, had toxoplasmosis at one point eighteen months before.

Toxoplasmosis is an illness well known in cats, sheep and humans and can cause abortions. 'Tis well known to spread by us felines as well as rodents and some even say by birds. Cats have traditionally been accused of being the terrible spreaders of toxoplasmosis. We allegedly hinder shepherds by infecting their flocks and ruining their health, so many sheep farmers intensely dislike us. With modern husbandry, however, the parasitic disease can be prevented by a vaccine or treated in humans with an antibiotic, if necessary. I help The Shepherd administer this vaccine every year, a month before our flock of ewes is visited by a ram. We use several vaccines, which keep our flock healthy. I feel that prevention is far better than cure, especially with sheep. Ask any shepherd and they will say that sheep seem to love to die in any way they can, even invent new ways to die. With farming livestock, one always has some dead stock and we mourn our losses of animal friends. By contrast there exists so much reward for us in all the wonderful real-world beauty that surrounds us and in life between birth and death: it keeps us going, ever hopeful and happy.

The Shepherd often tells me that her only companion during the years of bed rest that followed was her mind, filled with memories of her adventurous life. She couldn't watch TV or listen to music to distract herself as the noise and flickering light hurt her eyes and her head. So instead, she played out her recollections on the ceiling of her bedroom. She used the white cracked plaster as an imagined canvas where she painted her remembrances. At other times she closed her eyes and remembered in her mind's eye how she rode a horse galloping bareback by a sandy seashore. She sensed the inhalation of the smell and taste of wet salty sea air and the intimate feel of every one of her muscle movements staying with the motion of the horse. She felt the power, the wet and smell of horsey sweat and the lash of its mane whipping across her face as the horse rose and fell in its smooth soothing rocking rhythmic gallop. She recalled the sound and splash of hooves as they impacted the wave-washed sand and then pushed off to continue forward momentum.

The first year she mostly rested in bed to survive, but she planted an avocado seed, which she watched sprout and grow until it became so tall that it had to live outside her basement room's door in its second year. Then she was saddened when an early first frost killed it. Death was unintended, but these things happen.

As The Shepherd tells it, one of her most vivid memories of her years of bedridden stillness in Virginia, was lying on a sofa in her parents' sheltered glass sun porch, where she viewed a big Siberian Elm. This tree stood slightly downhill from the porch on the property line shared with the neighbours. What she remembers best is the many hours she lay each day watching the tree through all its seasons. So she can now see in retrospect a short film in her mind's eye of this great elm tree as it spun through its seasons of light spring green, summer's dark green, brown autumnal colours, the fall of leaves, then naked in winter, occasionally trimmed in snow or dripping icicles that glittered in winter sun.

When November rolls around, the coming of winter is in the air as frosts crunch underfoot. Final preparations must be made to house our ewes close to their lambing time so that their newborns will be sheltered from the worst weather. First, the shed must be cleared out and the floor cleaned of all manure. Then a layer of dried woodchips that The Shepherd received earlier in the year from a local tree surgeon is spread across the shed floor. Woodchips will insulate as well as absorb. Once they are spread, golden straw is rolled out on top of them. I LOVE this part as sometimes there are mice to chase when they come scuttling out of the straw. The straw is warm and insulates against the coming cutting winter winds. I am often found curled up in the straw bedding, as is Ovenmitt.

Once the lambing shed is prepared for winter, we are ready to bring in our expectant ewes. Having been introduced to the ram in October, they are now scanned with an ultrasound instrument to see how many lambs each ewe carries: one, two, three or none at all.

Lambing must be a carefully planned procedure and The Shepherd practises the modern husbandry technique of 'sponging' to ensure that all our ewes produce their lambs at more or less the same time. Such a tight breeding schedule enables The Shepherd to do all the lambing herself because she will have two precise sets of lambing dates with a ten-day break between each in the middle of the lambing season to recover from lack of sleep. Very sensible, I think.

Next, winter feeding begins and depends on such variables as when our ewes are due to lamb, how much grass is in our fields, how wet or dry our land is and the type of weather. Now I closely watch the condition of our rams' and ewes' feet – they are occasionally prone to scald. This condition is a bit like very severe athlete's foot in humans – except more painful than itchy, and can cause lameness. Ovenmitt often likes to sit and chat to The Shepherd when she has flipped over a sheep to tend to this bacterial problem. With a coarse cloth that she draws in between the sheep's cloven hoof, she cleans and dries each foot where the bacteria has rubbed and made the flesh raw. Then she sprays on a blue liquid spray that contains the antibiotic chlortetracycline, which kills and dries out the fungus. Within twenty-four hours the sheep is usually sound again.

Now is also the time that The Shepherd removes the ram after the six-week period he has had to be present during the two seventeen-day breeding cycles. When his work is done, he is placed in a confined space with all our other rams who have been taken away from their chosen flocks of ewes. They must be kept in this tightly confined space for a week to ten days so that they don't kill each other fighting over who is top boss.

As Black Sheep Farm is so hilly, a ram that charges downhill can easily hit and kill another ram. We all saw this happen once when The Shepherd turned our rams out together too early. I was, as usual, sitting on one of my fence posts, where I watched as the rams were turned out. One ram ran uphill, then turned and charged down, gathering speed as he went. Another ram, whom we call The Welshman, had faced uphill and stood his ground to challenge this act of aggression. The charging ram smashed right into him with such great force that The Welshman flipped over and flew backwards, knocked out cold. The Shepherd leapt into the field to chase off the aggressive ram, which was continuing to pummel the downed ram. She and her friends who had witnessed this thought he was surely dead as blood streamed from his nose. It took The Shepherd weeks of careful nursing to get The Welshman right again. She spent time and effort keeping him alive because she was fond of him and admired his hardy Zwartbles breeding from the Welsh Mountains. Happily, The Welshman survived, and The Shepherd had learned not to let rams out too early.

After rams get over their aggression towards each other, they and Smudge have a ten-month holiday to eat, sleep and enjoy a life of leisure till the next breeding season arrives.

With nights drawing in, there is more time to spend by the Aga to warm ourselves after our routine twice-daily feeding of hay and checking of stock. As daylight hours become so short and expectant ewes need eight hours between meals, our rounds are done after dark by torchlight or in light from the quad's headlights. In the mornings, as the darkness fades, the gloaming dawn light can be breathtakingly beautiful. The Shepherd stands to watch it unfold across the river valley as mists rise in cream greys, silvers, pinks and purples against the stark black-silhouetted winter trees. During these moments I must sometimes reach up and sink my claws into The Shepherd's leg to spur her into action as she stands transfixed. Our sheep must be fed, and our dogs are hungry, I want my second breakfast and she probably needs her pot of black tea and hot porridge.

On rainy mornings, I make my way across the yard as I hear The Shepherd perform her morning ablutions, brush her teeth, flush her litterbox, then thump downstairs to open the scullery door. As on every other morning, we felines are outside, waiting. We've hunted mice and rats all night while those canines had cushy beds in the farmhouse. I stretch my front paws as far up as I can reach on the red wooden scullery door to scratch my prime hunting talons with impatience. I hear a key click slowly in its lock. The Big Fellow finds the click unbearable, and lets out one of his rich, deep ear-splitting barks. Then the door opens and the dogs all rush past me as they leap over the threshold into the rain. I swish my tail that glitters with rain droplets, my wet coat sleeked down. Sauntering in, I leave wet paw prints on the scullery flagstones. I demand my first breakfast at once as I have worked hard all night. Ovenmitt bounds through the door after me, shaking rain off his short tabby coat, and tries to rub himself dry on The Shepherd's trousers. He plaintively mews complaints about all and sundry, as is his wont, and demands breakfast. A lidded bucket that holds our cat biscuits pops open and a scoop cut from a plastic milk carton digs out our breakfast biscuits.

As Ovenmitt and I settle into breakfast, all canines return with a bounce back inside. The Big Fellow whines impatiently as The Shepherd begins to pull on her boots, which Bear tries to grab at and run out the door into the rain with.

Finally, her boots are on and with a rustle the waterproof trousers are pulled up. Raincoat and hat are donned. With a pat on my back and a loving tug at Ovenmitt's tail, The Shepherd strides into wet and wind to do the morning rounds. With a bouncy meow, I trot behind her and try to keep up, my feline short-legged stride no match for her brisk walk, particularly when the yard is wet and muddy. I try to keep her abreast of the night's developments as she walks and as we begin another day.

The Shepherd often tells me stories by the Aga during the long winter nights – wild and colourful yarns about her former life as an actress, or learning to become a farmer. She has a couple of favourites, one involving someone she calls Ichabod Crane, a strange name, perhaps Dutch, I think, like the origins of my Zwartbles sheep. She often takes this story out for a spin at Hallowe'en. She tells me that the house where she lived, while breaking and training Morgan houses, in upstate New York, was once the home to a schoolteacher named Jesse Merwin, who would became known in the tale of the headless horseman as Ichabod Crane in *The Legend of Sleepy Hollow* by Washington Irving, an American writer.

The house was typically Dutch colonial, a wooden clapboard structure with big stone steps leading up to a small front porch. Large old trees surrounded the house and its small windows kept the interior cool during the height of summer. Offset and to the left was a more modern structure that housed a kitchen and another entrance, which was favoured over the traditional farmhouse front door. In farmhouses, you rarely, if ever, come in the front door anyway. Upon entering the kitchen extension, you could see three doors: one directly in front, which led out to the back of the house, a second on the far wall at an angle, which led down into the original house's root cellar and which would have been an exterior door before this kitchen had been built. As you turned right, you would reach a third door, which led to the old part of the house and the dining room. This room, too, had three doors, one on the opposite wall, which led into the rest of the house, to the owner's bedroom and to a snug living room. The second door opened into a small guest room with a bed, which was built into the original structure of the old house. The third door gave access to a steep narrow-walled stairway up to two bedrooms in the eves of the house. All doors in the old part of the house had traditional old metal hooks and latches, which made a double click and chink sound when they were opened and closed. Also, whenever a strong wind blew outside, they rattled.

The Shepherd stayed in a room at the top of those steep narrow stairs. One evening, when she returned from a 4th of July party on another farm, she entered the kitchen through the side entrance and locked its door. She noticed the open cellar door and light on. She walked over and called down to see if her boss was down below. There was no answer. She didn't want to turn off any lights if her boss was awake, as she was an elderly lady, so The Shepherd walked down into the cellar, but found no one. She came back upstairs and switched off the cellar light and closed the door. She stepped over the kitchen threshold into the dining room and switched off the kitchen light behind her.

As she was about to take another step she heard a door open and a light go on behind her. She turned, ready to apologise to her boss for turning the lights off prematurely, but no one was there. Confused, she went back into the kitchen, opened the cellar door and peered down. 'Hello?' No answer.

At this point The Shepherd thought perhaps the drink she had consumed at the party was playing tricks on her. She tiptoed across the house to her boss's bedroom and peered in to find her there safely fast asleep. So back into the kitchen she went, closed and latched the cellar door and turned off its light. Once again she crossed the dining room towards the latched door to the narrow steep stairs and her bedroom, but when she was halfway across the room, she heard the cellar door open again, but this time the kitchen light went on. The Shepherd beat a hasty retreat across the dining room to the door of the narrow steep stairs and up to the safety of her bedroom. She opened the latched door to the staircase, leapt through it, closing it hastily behind her and scurried up the stairs. She was hardly halfway up the stairs when the two doors at the foot of the stairs opened then closed, opened then closed, then began to latch and unlatch as if someone was on the other side of each door and opening and closing them rapidly. Every hair on her body stood on end, she told me, like a caricature Hallowe'en black cat. The Shepherd rushed up the remaining stairs, rounded the corner, leapt into bed, switched on the bedside light and stayed awake with goggle-eyed dread and fear all night. The next morning when The Shepherd smelled coffee and could hear her boss cooking the routine breakfast hamburger, she crept down-stairs with a bit less trepidation. Before she could ask anything, her boss thanked her for locking up and turning off all the lights. 'But ... but ... but ...' The Shepherd stumbled over the telling of her tale, recounting the opening and closing doors and the lights switching on and off by them-selves. 'Oh, that must have been Jesse Merwin playing a trick on you,' her boss laughed. 'Not to worry, he is very friendly and means no harm.' Needless to say, The Shepherd made sure she was exhausted every night after that so she could go to sleep with her lights on. What a scaredy-cat she was!

Her next favourite tale is one she calls *Deliverance*. I have never seen the film, but she tells me about a time when she lived in the Blue Ridge Mountains of Virginia riding horses long distances. Her friend at the time had what he called 'endurance horses' and they both worked to get them in shape to ride great distances. An able horsewoman, The Shepherd loved these long rides up into the Appalachian Mountains. If the dogs they rode with didn't stir far off the trails, she often saw lots of wildlife, flocks of wild turkey, deer, bobcats and brown bears.

On this particular day, they were out riding at the height of the bow-and-arrow hunting season in Virginia. This comes before the rifle-shooting season and enables local people to continue hunting for food such as wild turkeys, deer and bears, but on a more sustainable footing.

They had been riding for some hours with the dogs trotting a short distance ahead of them. Suddenly one dog leapt sideways, barking with fright, surprise and anger. At the same time The Shepherd's horse reared and spun, spooked. Not ten feet in front of them on the upper side of the trail's edge stood a fully camouflaged man, his face painted, and armed with a bow and arrow. Further along, but down the steep slope, was a second man camouflaged from head to foot but armed with a hunting rifle, which this early in the hunting season was illegal. Sensibly, The Shepherd and her companion rode on as quietly and quickly as possible down the mountain, doubling back onto a different route to head home. A few miles further on, they came to a mountain stream that tumbled down between rocky outcrops. As they carefully crossed the rocky mountain stream, they heard a noise. They looked up to see the two well-armed men standing upstream on boulders looking down on them as their horses picked their way across the stream, their weapons trained on the two riders. Outflanked and outarmed, The Shepherd and her companion rode away as quickly as they could. They had angered the hunters by disturbing their stalking of whatever quarry they had been pursuing.

It makes me grateful for my small plot of land by the banks of the River Nore. There are no men armed with bows and arrows or big cougars calling in these green fields, just the baa of the chocolate-coloured sheep, birds singing and occasional fox barks, with the blue of the Blackstairs Mountains visible in the distance.

11
Christmas at Black Sheep Farm

As December deepens, the pinnacle of shorter days and longer nights approaches. The winter solstice, the shortest day of the year, lands on the twenty-first day of December. By my sheep-leg-count calculation, that's about five and one quarter of one sheep.

Most years, after our wintry lunch of hot soup or stew, The Shepherd and I walk out with our canine crew to find and select a small branch of holly heavy with bright red berries and also a small oak tree branch with healthy buds on it for the expedition to celebrate the winter solstice. When we are out picking these branches, Pepper gets very excited and his back legs start to vibrate in anticipation, as he knows they will soon be off on an adventure. However, Pepper hardly ever barks, reserving his deep, low 'woof' for badgers, foxes and the occasional stranger who calls in at the farm.

He is intelligent enough to know the difference between the noises car engines make, and when it's The Shepherd's, he doesn't make a sound.

Holly and oak represent folklore and mythology of the battle between the Holly and Oak kings for supremacy, as the year wheels slowly from season to season. One monarch rules the waxing year, the other the waning year. Winter and summer solstices have critical importance as longest night and longest day respectively. The battle between the kings happens each year during the equinox of equal day and night as the seasons turn. At the peak of extremely long summer light (the longest day), or at the very depth of dark winter (the shortest day), one king is strongest.

The Holly King rules at the height of his power during the winter solstice before longer days commence with more light and rebirth of the shining sun that gives life to the Earth. With the warmth of spring, the Oak King's sap begins to flow, his buds burst, leaves unfurl and flowers appear. With summer solstice, the King Oak tree rules supreme as he has spread his strong green leaves widely and begins to ripen his acorn fruit. Come the summer equinox in June, the Oak King remains dominant. Hints of coming winter appear in September when the Oak King's leaves begin to curl a bit with brown edges as he prepares to shed his mighty crown of leaves and drop acorns at his feet. Once again the Holly King assumes the ruling mantle as his spiky green leaves shine brightly in the September sun and his green berries start to swell and slowly turn to red.

On the day of the winter solstice The Shepherd gathers together an assortment of human friends as well as Pepper, who has always loved adventures off the farm. Personally, I prefurrr to stay on the farm. After a long drive up narrow winding country roads, they park and gather at the foot of a hill above the village of Tullaghought. They start to hike up a long, tortuous, muddy and stony boreen (which is what narrow country roads are called in this part of the world), with high hedges on either side, until they reach a mesh-covered gate. They climb over the gate and heft Pepper over as it is usually locked. Next, they have to walk around a wide shallow pond that is sometimes frozen. If the ice is thick enough, humans throw stones that skip on it to make a funny thwock, thwock, thwack, sound. Pepper says it's like skipping stones because of the way they jump across the ice. He enjoys the chase of these stones but is careful if the ice is too thin.

As their uphill hike progresses, they pass through an old farmyard with tumbledown moss-covered ruins of stone buildings. After slogging through the muddy farmyard they push uphill and round a corner through a tree-shrouded lane sided by stone walls thick with moss and ferns. They perse-vere up a steeper part of the hill through a field and over the crest of the topmost ridge, where they arrive at the flat space of the Baunfree Passage Tomb.

Baunfree is a stone circle on a small plateau with spectacular views of South Kilkenny, East Tipperary and Waterford.
Recently, as planted woodlands have grown taller, you can
no longer view the sea beyond Waterford. The group arrive
just before sunset. The Shepherd places her small branch of
berried holly and her fat-budded oak branch on top of one
of the highest standing stones as a tribute to the people who
built this ancient monumental circle. Then she opens her
thermos flask of homemade hot chocolate and pours everyone a steaming tin mug. Together they raise their mugs to
toast the coming of the New Year when the sun starts to
lengthen daylight. Pepper loves this expedition because
when he is up on the hilltop he can stand, sniff the air and
smell all the scents of what has happened that day wafting
up from miles around. When he comes home to Black Sheep
Farm, he tells me all about it and I can't help but feel a dart
of envy that The Shepherd doesn't invite me to be part of
this ritual.

Pepper tells me that when darkness falls, they hike down
by torchlight to their cars and drive to a village pub, where
they warm themselves with hot port. Along the way they
pass a house covered with every sort of Christmas light
you can imagine. So they have savoured two very different
Irish worlds: the beautiful ancient ruins where long-gone
tribes once worshipped the return of the sun's earliest
lengthening of daylight contrast harshly with the black

night pierced by blazing decorative modern electric lights of many colours.

In other years, I believe, their winter solstice pilgrimage has taken them to the passage tomb of Knockroe, a Neolithic ceremonial location which nestles on a south-facing slope of Kilmacoliver Hill. The tomb's westward view aligns its stones with midwinter's setting sun, towards the mountain of Slievenamon in County Tipperary. If the winter weather is not too cloudy to block sunlight, as the sun sets it casts a beam between two decorated carved stones to the back of the passage tomb.

This winter solar phenomenon is similar to those at Newgrange, Knowth and Loughcrew passage tombs. Newgrange is probably the best-known of these, as the mid-winter sun rises and pierces the depth of the tomb, but Knockroe is one of the most decorated tombs outside the Boyne Valley and in recent years winter solstice crowds have greatly enlarged at Knockroe, so it has become much more difficult to see this wondrous sight on 21 December.

Once, long ago, when The Shepherd was a small child, she tells me that she was taken to picnic on top of Newgrange with her grandfather, sister, a cousin and some of her grandfather's friends. Archaeologists had begun to work on restoring this ancient monument site well before there were many visitors. Since the surrounding fields were filled with nettles and thistles, they had sat on top of the grass-covered

Newgrange mound munching well-buttered bread covered with sliced red tomatoes picked fresh from Black Sheep Farm's vegetable garden that morning.

As they picnicked, several archaeologists sensed these visitors were quite interested in Newgrange and inquired if The Shepherd's grandfather would like to climb down a ladder to see inside another ancient mound. He replied that he would like that very much indeed. The Shepherd scampered quickly after her grandfather and clambered down the ladder into the dark tomb chamber below. From the entrance hole above their heads the archaeologist shone his torchlight to illuminate some of the features.

Most of the historical archaeological conversation sailed over The Young Shepherd's head, but it was a memorable adventure. They climbed out and followed the archaeologist into a second tunnel, where they walked to the back of the inner passage to view a huge stone bowl that filled the excavated space.

The archaeologist suggested to The Young Shepherd: 'Go now and sit in that big bowl, for you will probably be the last child ever to have the pleasure of sitting in it. We are about to install bars across the entrance to the chamber to keep the bowl safe from vandals.' The Shepherd remembers well that she sat with her skinny legs tucked beneath her thin body against the smooth cold carved stone of this huge ancient bowl and looked out the entrance passage towards the bright light of a summer's day. This bowl had been placed in the tomb before the narrow passageway had been made as it was physically impossible to have put in the bowl after the passage had been built. So as a child, The Shepherd had sat in an ancient carved Stone Age bowl that was older than the pyramids of Egypt.

Christmas-morning stars shine sharp and bright in a black, crisp, moonless sky. All is quiet as only a distant fox, a vixen in her three-day heat, screams her shrill call for a mate, and frost thickens its grasp on the fields' grassy stems in the pre-dawn gloaming.

Lambing time is when we are all in the sheep shed watching, waiting and anticipating the birth of our new season's lambs. I have my full winter coat fluffed out as insulation against the cold, always on watch and keeping The Shepherd company. Ovenmitt, my Shepherd Cat apprentice, also appears and will sit on The Shepherd's lap. Ovenmitt then climbs onto the back of a friendly ewe who has come to lie down near The Shepherd's feet and unintentionally warm her toes. To survive the cold, The Shepherd sips a mug of tea clasped tightly to keep her hands warm and waits to see if she is needed. We are all watching a ewe who is about to lamb. All is quiet, only the rustle of straw as the lambing ewe circles and paws the ground in anticipation of her first lamb. Both Ovenmitt and I purr in the comfort of companionable company. The rest of the flock are all cosy in straw sleeping or methodically quietly chewing their cuds. Time continues gently to weave its way through these calm moments of reflection. It helps to strengthen a pattern woven into the fabric that is our life; it enables us to absorb frenetic events that occur throughout one's lifetime.

Leading up to Christmas, The Shepherd always worries about there not being enough eggs for eggnog. During the winter months, egg-makers always lay fewer eggs with cold weather's much-shorter hours of daylight. They enter a rest period or egg-laying hibernation. So The Shepherd collects those few eggs and guards them jealously for a festive Christmas morning when her nearby cousins and house guests gather for homemade eggnog.

When the house fills with friends and relations a few days before Christmas, there is usually a kitchen party making Christmas tree decorations. Coloured paper chains have been a longstanding tradition in the house, with popcorn and cranberry chains added to the decor in more recent years.

We all go into the fields and walk along the hedgerows to collect holly and ivy to decorate the house. The Shepherd and I usually watch through the autumnal months to ascertain where holly berries are thickest. We only hope hungry birds don't eat them before Christmas decoration time.

Christmas time also brings back sad memories for The Shepherd as her granny died three days before Christmas

1996. Then, it was the first time The Shepherd had returned to Ireland after her bout with tropical illness. She returned with her mother and father, even though she had to be moved through airports in a wheelchair as she was still very weak from her three-year illness.

As a passenger during the dawn-dark drive from Dublin Airport through the Irish winter countryside, The Shepherd tried to sit erect in the car to watch the winter-sleeping farmland roll past her window, but she became too exhausted. She lay flat in the back seat so she could only smell the countryside as they travelled south to County Kilkenny. She detected the distinctive odours of farming, especially the molasses-sweetened, fermented aroma of silage as farmers fed their sheep and cattle in the early-morning light. As they drew closer to home, they passed through villages with people awakening and lighting their fires. The pleasant pungent smell of turf smoke seeped through the car's closed windows, another sensory welcome back to Ireland for The Shepherd after her long absence in New York and then in London and in the Far East, before she returned to her parents' home in Virginia to recuperate. To The Shepherd, they were the smells of home.

The next day, refreshed from her long sleep, The Shepherd and her father drove to the hospital to visit her granny. She lay there in her hospital bed, eyes closed, breathing easily, seemingly in comfort of a restful sleep. The Shepherd asked a nurse if her granny could wake up or if she would know that The Shepherd was there. The nurse replied that the last thing to go at this stage was hearing so that she should talk to her granny and let her know she was there. The Shepherd sat in a chair next to her bed and reached over to take her hand, which lay warm across her crisp white hospital sheets. She held her granny's hand and sat quietly for a little while just holding her hand, allowing a lifetime of memories to surge through her mind.

The last time The Shepherd had seen her granny had been three years earlier when she had been brought home to Black Sheep Farm still very ill, as a stopover on her journey from London back to her parents' home in the USA. Her granny, despite her overwhelmingly painful arthritic knees and hips, struggled upstairs every day to visit The Shepherd in her bedroom. The Shepherd lay in that bed for a month, listening to house life and distant farm noises. Wind and rain beat upon the bedroom window, dogs barked and far-off cows lowed as they anticipated their feed. She heard cawing crows leave their roosts in the trees beside the house each morning as they announced to the world they had departed their tree-top bedchambers with loud caustic cackling. Then, on still days, when no wind or rain rattled the old glass window sashes, she could hear them return to their roost in a flurry of flapping wings and loud cackling as they gossiped before settling down for the night.

She wished she had enough strength to go downstairs and sit in the room by the log fire with her granny but the grip of her illness kept her immobile, so in the bed she stayed. Her ma carried logs and turf bricks upstairs and lit and tended the fire in her bedroom, but her company was her own for many hours each day.

As her recollections progressed, The Shepherd began to speak to her granny, who lay so still in her hospital bed. As The Shepherd sat there, her father moved off to discuss her granny's illness with the doctors who were looking after her. Granny was a religious sort, who loved classical music and singing hymns in church. While The Shepherd rarely attended church, she had memorised a few hymns and spirituals. She chose to sing an old African-American spiritual. She recalled that her granny had often mentioned how others had crossed over Jordan. She hummed an introduction at first and then sang low and soft as she leaned in towards her granny's ear so that only she could hear the lyrics and so as not to perturb nurses, doctors or other patients in other rooms on the hospital floor.

Swing low, sweet chariot,
Coming for to carry me home.
Swing low, sweet chariot,
Coming for to carry me home

I looked over Jordan, what did I see,
Coming for to carry me home.
A band of angels coming for me,
Coming for to carry me home.

Swing low, sweet chariot,
Coming for to carry me home.
Swing low, sweet chariot,
Coming for to carry me home.

If you get there before I do,
Coming for to carry me home.
Tell all my friends I'm coming, too,
Coming for to carry me home.

As The Shepherd sang this song she felt an ever-so-slight movement in the hand she held. Had Granny heard the song? Did she know The Shepherd was there? She strengthened the depth and volume of her voice. As she continued to sing, she saw tears run from beneath her granny's eyelids that were closed against the bright winter-morning light. The tears trickled down her pale cheeks as she lay so still. While The Shepherd awaited her father's return, she sang her granny's favourite song, one she'd often sung to The Shepherd and her siblings when they were children. To this day The Shepherd's musical memory hears her granny's voice singing this young maiden's folk song:

I am a young maiden and my story is sad
For once I was courted by a brave sailor lad.
He courted me strongly by night and by day
But now my dear sailor has gone far away.

(Chorus) If I were a blackbird, I'd whistle and sing
And I'd follow the ship that my true love sails in
And on the top rigging I'd there build my nest
And I'd pillow my head on his lily-white breast.
He promised to take me to Donnybrook fair
To buy me red ribbons to tie up my hair
And when he'd return from the ocean so wide
He'd take me and make me his own loving bride.

If I were a blackbird, I'd whistle and sing
And I'd follow the ship that my true love sails in
And on the top rigging I'd there build my nest
And I'd pillow my head on his lily-white breast.

His parents they slight me and will not agree
That me and my sailor boy married will be
But when he comes home, I will greet him with joy
And I'll take to my heart my dear sailor boy.

Once the song had been sung, a settled stillness of quiet calm filled the air. The Shepherd's memories flooded back to her: being surrounded with tin buckets brimming with fresh-cut flowers from the garden, the air saturated with fragrance of all sorts, like sweet Williams, tea roses and sweet peas. Her granny had sung as they both tied bunches of flowers up with raffia to sell at the local country market the next day.

The Shepherd's father returned to the room and told her that they would come back for an afternoon visit. They left the hospital for Black Sheep Farm to have lunch and collect The Shepherd's mother for their afternoon visit at the hospital. As they drove into the farmyard, Mother came out to meet them: 'I just had a call from the hospital. They told me that Mama just died. They said she died very soon after you left.' Filled with emotion, The Shepherd felt very glad and very sad, glad that she had been able to spend time with her granny before she had died and sing her both songs.

The day before Christmas they buried her granny next to her grandfather in the graveyard of the small church where several generations of her family had been buried, where The Shepherd's parents had married and where The Shepherd was christened. They kept that Christmas very simple. No presents were exchanged among immediate family. Many friends invited them to family feasts but they preferred to remain at Black Sheep Farm and dine upon gifts that many friends and relations brought to their house. They had brought fresh eggs, a bottle of champagne and a smoked salmon. Others brought newly home-baked bread, milk and a pot of homemade jam. Their Christmas Day began with a breakfast of toast, jam and strong Barry's Tea. The holiday dinner was simply scrambled eggs, smoked salmon with capers and champagne. Together they walked around the farm, took in fresh air and did not fuss about a grand meal; they were just family quietly held together.

Some years Christmas can be very busy and incredibly complex as The Shepherd and I lamb sheep as well as prepare and celebrate festive feasts. With these intermixed events The Shepherd may be late to the meal because a ewe is lambing, but she always goes out between courses to check if any ewe threatens to lamb on Christmas Day. If the house is fully occupied on Christmas Day and a ewe starts to lamb, everybody puts on boots to come out to witness the new birth. After the lamb has safely entered this world and is suckling her mother ewe, the inhabitants of the house return to dine and celebrate the new life born on such a festive day.

As The Shepherd's family is half-American, Christmas isn't as big an affair as Thanksgiving, but food is still central to the Christmas celebrations. Traditionally, The Shepherd's family begin with fresh, homemade eggnog laced with brandy on Christmas morning with friends and relations who visit. Their main meal of the day begins with smoked salmon on brown bread and their bird of choice depends on numbers of family or guests who will be coming to dinner. Some years, there's duck when there are few for the meal, and when there are bigger numbers, a turkey, and a goose if numbers fall in between. Vegetables are roast potatoes, Brussels sprouts with walnuts, gravy and finally, a flaming Christmas pudding with lashings of brandy butter.

The family has only twice departed from their age-old traditions: when Granny died, and during the Big Freeze in 2010, when the pipes froze and there was no water or central heating. The Shepherd and the guests had to draw water from the aquifer spring across the fields and carry buckets to the house and stable. The Shepherd still remembers the sight of the steam rising from the warm spring water into the icy air when all around was frozen solid. She also remembers fondly the paper plates and cups they used for Christmas dinner that year, as washing up wasn't a possibility. Sometimes it's the Christmases that depart from tradition that we remember, for happy reasons and for sad.

The Shepherd often takes a party of guests to ring in the New Year at Saint Canice's, the cathedral that stands on a hill overlooking my city of Kilkenny. They sup on a big bowl of The Shepherd's homemade bean-and-mince chilli with rice, then set off for the half-hour drive into the city and arrive at the cathedral at about 11.30. Once inside the cathedral, they follow the bell-ringers through a small door and ascend the narrow winding stone steps worn from centuries of feet climbing up into the bell tower. They step through a door into the tolling room, where bell ropes hang down from holes in the ceiling. As midnight approaches, bell-ringers ring out the old year with padded bell clappers, which mute the tone into muffled rings at the dying of the old year. Then, five minutes before midnight, several bell-ringers scurry up more stone steps and through a narrow door, out into the open air onto the cathedral's roof, which they cross to then descend through a wooden-slatted flap into the bell room, where they take off the bells' leather muffles. As the countdown commences the caller counts down for the bell-puller of the striking bell, 'Three, two, one ...', and the bell-puller pulls the rope and the bell's wheel starts to turn as he or she cries, 'Going, going, gone' as the bell rings the hour. After twelve strikes, a caller calls out which bell is to be pulled next and soon the ringing music of bells can be heard across the city from St Canice's and all other church towers that have joined, ringing into the crisp midnight air.

As the old year is rung out, the new one starts with more lambs arriving at all hours of the day and night. Some winters can be bitterly cold, but this is also when the Zwart-bles' docility and rich milk are a great boon, when one needs the colostrum, a mother's warm golden first milk, to feed those newborn lambs in difficulty. When during Christmas 2010, icy weather froze all our water pipes and The Shepherd was forced to haul water buckets from our aquifer spring to the livestock, winds became so bitterly cold that fresh-born wet lambs exposed to freezing air became hypothermic quickly. The Shepherd rubbed the newborns dry with fresh straw, milked ewes and then tubed colostrum into lambs. To tube a lamb, she had to insert a thin long tube into the mouth down into their stomach and to make sure it bypassed the lungs. Once the tube was correctly inserted, The Shepherd poured colostrum into a syringe and pushed the syringe plunger so the milk went down the tube into the lamb's stomach.

To counteract hypothermia in the lambs, she hung heat lamps in the shed and moved wet newborn lambs into the Aga's bottom-left oven to dry and warm the lambs. At her busiest there were three lambs at a time being warmed and dried in the bottom oven and two beneath heat lamps out of that life-killing bitterly cold wind. This benchmark winter of cold-weather lambing always makes us hope for normal Irish mild weather – which doesn't mean there aren't other trying episodes to be had while our flock is lambing.

It's nearly twenty years ago now, but if I ask her, The Shepherd will try to remember the early days at Black Sheep Farm. A few months after Granny died and spring had arrived, The Shepherd decided that she would return to Ireland and try to live permanently on Black Sheep Farm. When she first returned she was still too weak to farm but she could walk into the overgrown garden, which was a jungle of brambles, nettles and self-sown ash saplings, and where she found the abandoned rhubarb patch and picked stems to stew. She discovered self-sown ragged cabbages to harvest, which she would fry in butter with caraway seeds and toasted sesame seed oil. She also picked young nettles, which she steamed or made into soup. During that year's summer months she found soft fruits – raspberries, goose-berries, loganberries and black- and redcurrants – were hidden beneath years of overgrowth. All berries were eaten or cooked into jams, or stewed and frozen for later use. In the autumn, apple, fig, pear and plum trees were laden with fruit and the hazel tree branches weighed down with nuts. Again she grazed her way among the plentiful ripe fruits. She picked, cooked and stewed her bounty to stock the freezer and make jams. After a while she gathered enough strength to start to clear areas of the garden. She pruned trees that had not been pruned in over twenty years. She chopped out dead wood as she had learned from her grandfather.

Since she had returned to Ireland during the late spring, The Shepherd had only mild-weather clothing to wear. As winter approached, old friends kindly gave her their cast-off winter clothing and she began to settle into life on Black

Sheep Farm. The Shepherd had learned the skill of photography during her many years away from the farm. After eighteen months of continued slow recovery and modestly increasing vigour, she managed to get a job teaching photography in Kilkenny city and Thomastown. The following spring, the curly-haired farmer gave her the first of his triplets of pet lambs from his ewes' spring crop and her new ovine life began. At this stage, the farm fields were rented by a neighbouring farmer and so, using pallets, she fenced parts of the garden and lawns around the house to make grass paddocks for the new sheep to graze in. As her strength slowly continued to increase, she returned to the seasonal rhythms of farm life. As her flock enlarged, the farmer who had rented the land eventually departed and she took up the reins, managing all the green small fields around the house, the farmyards and the orchard.

12
The Virus Threatens

January is the time for winter lambing. The Shepherd has many years' experience of lambing and often tells me about the period in 1982, which I mentioned earlier, when she spent time on a farm in Wicklow, working seven days a week with only one day off during the entire time she was there.

An au pair lived on this farm, too, and one day, she invited The Shepherd on a trip to Dublin, announcing that she planned to have a manicure there at a posh shopping centre. The Shepherd looked down at her hands, ingrained with dirt, the lines and crevices grubby from weeks of lambing ewes, but she agreed to go. A manicure might be just the thing, she thought, to repair the damage of many weeks' hard work. When she got there, she showed the manicurist her hands, asking, 'What can you do with these?' The woman blanched. 'Oh, I can't do anything for those hands! The only thing I can recommend you do is cover them in Vaseline and wrap them in plastic bags while you have a good hot bath.'

Vanity has never been part of The Shepherd's makeup – life on the farm doesn't require much in the way of stylish clothing and so she wears practical, warm clothes, her grey mane tied back in a ponytail and well out of her way while she walks the fields with me as we check the flock.

As lambing progresses through the month, I can be found out in the sheep shed sitting on a round bale of hay. It is calm out of the wind and weather, but the shed fills with fresh air as it has an open side facing a hill. Our shed has slowly taken form over many years. When The Shepherd came home, it was a mucky corner of our Wind-Charger Field with old stone walls on two sides, rotten wooden posts, knitted together with spiderwebs, holding up a tin roof; 'twas more like a colander than a shelter from wet weather. Beside it was a towering pile of rubble, stones, bricks, rusty pipes, fencing wire with rotten stakes attached, and rusty pieces of old shed roof. It was covered in thistles, nettles and clumps of tough coarse grass, but lambs still loved to dance, run and romp up it to play 'King of the Mountain'.

A time came when our ancient lean-to shed was pulled down. The dirt floor was dug out, a gravel drain and gravel floor put in, new steel piers were erected and a new tin roof hammered into place. That first year of the two-bay shed was wonderful for ewes and lambs to shelter in. A small retaining wall at one end had been built so there could be a level floor: it held the uphill side of the field at bay. Lambs loved to run about inside and out of the shed, race up the small rise, then jump down off the retaining wall into a bed of clean dry straw. They would gallop in circles and frolic whenever their mothers ate their meals. The Shepherd would lean back against the wall like a flamingo on one leg bent at the knee, her foot flat on the wall, making a purrrrfect half lap-cat shelf for me to jump up on to watch lambs frolic without the danger of my tail being mistakenly stomped on.

Over the years the shed was extended and a cement floor laid out with a small fenced yard to work with sheep when vaccinating, dosing, shearing, tagging, weaning, selling or treating them for any ailments. So now, with two solid walls, a wind-break slatting made from wood on its far end, I help to oversee The Shepherd. 'Tis the purrrrfect location on the farm for lambing in winter months. With enough fresh air no sheep will overheat, and as long as no biting wind blows directly into the shed from the northeast, the lambs stay cosy in deep straw near their warm woolly mothers.

There used to be a comfortable old chair in the shed, with wooden arms and legs covered in ancient, green horse-hair-stuffed upholstery. I could curl up in it during lambing time or share it with The Shepherd while we waited for a ewe to lamb. One summer a visitor fell in love with it, so The

Shepherd's mother gave it away. She didn't realise 'twas our well-loved comfortable lambing chair as it just looked sad and neglected, dust clinging to spun cobwebs in a corner of the shed's shadowed light. There is a photo somewhere of a young Pepper seated on it as he took his turn to watch over sheep in the days when our lamb pens were made out of salvaged wood pallets.

Way back, when lambing used to happen later in spring, we were feeding sheep in the field when The Shepherd noticed that a Suffolk Texel cross had no interest in food. She continually licked her lips, a clear sign that she was about to lamb. Now, if you'll remember, this large white ewe was our famous Great White Yoke, because of her independent mind. I helped The Shepherd to separate her from the main flock in the field and we brought her into the shed. She would become our first of the flock to lamb that year, so we all hoped birthing would go well. The Shepherd had bred this ewe to my Zwartbles ram and so we expected twin lambs at least. Over the previous few years this particular ewe had always lambed without problems. She always lambed down on her own, had at least twin lambs and raised them with distinction.

After a few hours we saw the first lamb sack begin to appear, so we knew birthing was imminent. Half an hour later, the birth bag burst, but we could still see nothing. The

Shepherd inspected the birth canal and found two hind legs inside. This birth position is quite dangerous. When a lamb comes out backwards, it often breathes in before it has fully emerged from the ewe's birthing canal. The danger is the lamb may drown itself by inhaling its birth fluid. So The Shepherd grabbed the lamb's two hind legs and pulled it from the birth canal as quickly as possible. Sadly, the fine-sized ram lamb had died.

In a flash The Shepherd swiftly reached inside to look for the twin, who was also presenting backwards. She promptly pulled out the live spluttering twin, then cleared the second ram lamb's face of birth fluid and put him in front of the ewe so she could start to clean and bond with it. Then she eased her hands deep into the ewe's uterus to check if there was yet another lamb – and discovered a triplet. The Shepherd felt it wriggling, definitely not a good sign because the triplet might drown by breathing in birth fluid. It was backwards, too, so as fast as she could, The Shepherd rapidly extracted the third lamb. She hastily cleared its airway and then gripped its back legs, spun herself around and swung the triplet like the end of wheel-spoke to thrust more inhaled fluid out of its lungs. After a few spins we saw the last lamb was a baby ewe and she began to breathe well. The Shepherd rubbed her and her brother vigorously with fresh clean straw to dry and stimulate them to move. She left them both breathing easily, with heads up and making small bleats while The Great White Yoke licked them clean and happily muttered to them in a motherly bonding way.

As The Shepherd and I departed from the birthing shed, she remarked how it was, 'So boring to birth backwards triplets. With such bad luck one might lose the second living lamb even after spinning it like a helicopter rotor.'

While inside its mother's uterus a lamb grows normally, floating around in a warm sea of fluid protecting it from potential bumps. The danger appears as the time of birth approaches. If a lamb has not sorted itself out to dive, front hooves first, with its head nestled at the knees, down the birth canal but is turned, to emerge hind legs first, the potential fatal inhaling of birth fluid is heightened. It will very likely die when it breathes in its birth fluid unless immediate preventive action is taken. Spinning a back-legs-first lamb like a helicopter propeller means holding its hind legs while swinging it in a circle. The centrifugal force of the spin pushes inhaled birth liquid out of its lungs. I strongly recommend that you duck away when the lamb is spun unless you don't mind being sprayed by gloopy birth fluid that flies out of the lungs. Ovenmitt once got a right big gob of it in his face when he tried to help The Shepherd by batting at the front legs of a lamb with his paws as she swung it past the hay bale he sat on.

When I returned later with The Shepherd to examine the lambs' progress, we found the ram lamb standing up and looking for a suckle from The Great White Yoke. Unfortunately, our ewe lamb had not risen up – she was still collapsed and getting colder. We rubbed her vigorously again with straw. Then The Shepherd turned her over to help the ewe lamb suckle colostrum directly from her mother's teat. She knelt behind the ewe and had the ewe's woolly back leaning against her front. That way she had the ewe sit on her bottom with all her legs in the air. When held correctly, any ewe will relax into the person holding them. With one hand she laid the ewe lamb across that comfortable area of wool-less warm skin between our ewe's back leg and stomach, so that the lamb's head pointed towards her mother's teats. She then reached around to gently pull one of the ewe's teats to break the waxy seal and make sure milk would flow easily. Once this was done she brought her ewe lamb's head towards the milky teat while holding the teat with her second hand. She worked her pinkie finger into the lamb's mouth to open it to take in the teat. Once the teat was inserted into the lamb's mouth, she helped the lamb by milking the teat directly into the lamb, who started swallowing right away. This would warm the baby ewe and give her strength to move her legs and stand on her own. She seemed better, so The Shepherd left again, but when she came back for the half-hour check, she found the lamb shivering. She placed a heat lamp nearby to warm her but still kept her close to her mother, The Great White Yoke.

Later that night I came with The Shepherd for evening rounds and to check on our season's first new lambs. Unhappily, we found our ewe lamb in a very bad way. She had just about stopped shivering, her mouth was stone cold and her breathing sounded like a death rattle. Hypothermia had set in. Only one more try at lifesaving treatment remained for her and for us. We had to warm her as quickly as possible. So we brought her into the kitchen and grabbed the nearest newspaper, which happened to be that week's *Irish Farmers Journal*. We spread it over her as a blanket and we placed her in the warming oven of the Aga.

We sat all night next the cooker warming the 'Aga Lamb'. Oscar and I rotated our watch from the Aga top. He even slid into the oven to add his body heat to the baby ewe lamb's and to boost her warming-up process.

After a while we three noticed that the lamb had stopped shivering, even bleated a few times and tried to stand. But we popped her back in the oven because The Shepherd felt her mouth was still too cold.

Sometime after 2 a.m. The Shepherd thought the lamb was going to live. She tucked the baby ewe into a dog cage full of straw bedding right next to the Aga. So off to bed The Shepherd went after she'd ushered both Oscar and myself outside into the icy-cold night air. We raced to the loose hay piled in the stable to stay warm and to watch for any stray rat or mouse to hunt or amuse ourselves with. 'Twas such a long night with not a mouse or a rat to entertain us. We had to wait till morning to see if our first ewe lamb of the season had outlived the night. Miraculously, she survived, thanks to our team's care, which boded well for the rest of that year's lambing season.

We put our three heads together. What should we name her after our and her strenuous night's labour? We decided we should call her Aggee, the Aga lamb, since into our heads bobbed up her purrfect nickname: Aggee. Still here on the farm, Aggee produces her own lambs every year. Aggee is the one grown-up ewe I greet with a gentle headbutt, as long as other ewes don't show their jealousy when I show my favouritism.

Now that we lamb in January, not that much has changed, but the first month of the year is that frightening time when the cycle of Schmallenberg virus (SBV) damage may become evident in the lambing flock. SBV is named after the beautiful German village of Schmallenberg, where the virus was first discovered. It causes deformities in newborn lambs or calves. I well recall the time I helped The Shepherd to birth an SBV-damaged lamb. It was late on a cold January night … this night was not just cold, but bitter icy cold. The wind even cut through my thick fur, so I was inside, cosily, with my coat fluffed, curled up in the barn's pile of sweet-smelling hay with my eyes closed, listening for rodents stirring.

I heard the back door to the farmhouse close and I wandered outside to see The Shepherd walking across the yard towards the sheep shed, her head bent against the wind. She huddled inside many layers of winter clothes. I inhaled the crisp air and it made me feel alive. The sky looked as if a cat like me had kneaded its claws in a black velvet cloth, leaving holes for starlight to leak through. I watched, yawned, stretched, wiped my face and then proceeded after her towards the sheep shed. Duty called.

I caught up with The Shepherd just as she reached the first set of gates. I let her know that I was there, and that I could ably assist or give helpful instructions. As she opened the gate and walked through, I followed, chatting to her in my own language, which after so many years she understands. I informed her that no mice or rats had yet appeared this evening, but I'd come out with her to the lambing shed to see if any sheep were lambing. I had missed the earlier inspection, so I didn't know that she'd already had her eye on a ewe that had given early warning signs that she might lamb later tonight.

We arrived at the lambing shed and the sheep stirred. The Shepherd had left on the lights continuously rather than flicking lights on and off so as not to frighten the ewes if they were asleep. Besides, this lights-on at lambing time helps immensely with my hunting of rats and mice, making it doubly handy.

We both spotted the ewe who was lambing and we instinctively knew something didn't seem right. As I watched from outside the large lambing pen, I let The Shepherd know that she should move the ewe quietly into a small pen to make it easier for her to help the ewe to birth. As soon as she had the ewe penned, she went off to get the lambing bucket, which held all the necessary tools for complicated lambing. My instinct told me that we were in for a night of it, so I trotted over and sat in my favourite place in the corner of the pen. I put my back against the stone wall so that none of the other ewes could sneak up behind me to sniff and flooff with my tail, which they love doing but which annoys me very much.

When The Shepherd brought the lambing bucket back, she stepped into the pen, quickly caught the lambing ewe and turned her on her side. The ewe was doing everything that we'd expect in a normal lambing: rapidly licking her lips in anticipation of cleaning her newborn lamb, stretching her neck and body, pushing and calling out with a strangled 'baa' as her natural lambing contractions began. As I watched this scene, The Shepherd said, 'Yes, I know, I know; something is *so* not right, Bodacious.'

As we were sheltered from direct wind in the lambing shed, The Shepherd took off her outer coat and draped it across the far corner of the pen, at some distance from me. I was annoyed because she didn't think I might like to sit on it to keep it warm for her. I had to tell her off, walking along the wooden pen fence to the corner and sitting on her warm coat. I managed to forget for a moment about the other ewes potentially sniffing my tail. These lambing events were far more important and possibly very complicated.

Lambing can be a messy business, so reader beware – but The Shepherd and I have been doing it for so many years now that we've grown used to it and understand that it's all part of a natural process. The life cycle exists in the sheep world, just as in the human. So, after putting lubrication gel all over her right hand, The Shepherd reached inside the ewe's birthing passage and found it only partly widened for lamb birth.

'Oh dear, Bodacious, this does not look good!!' There was a deep sigh, then a grrrrrring sound from The Shepherd. Something had most definitely gone wrong.

'Why, oh why, did it have to be this sheep?' she said. This was a ewe of high quality and new to my flock. It came to us pregnant by a ram unrelated to any other sheep here on the farm. We wanted to strengthen our breeding programme by producing offspring unrelated to our other ewes, so we hoped it would have at least one ram lamb. This would help broaden the genetic mix and improve my flock of purebred sheep.

The Shepherd explored inside the ewe's uterus with her hand, trying to find a way to help pull the lamb out. She massaged the entranceway to widen the opening to where the lamb lay inside. This took time because The Shepherd must pull as the ewe pushes, the two working in tandem to stimulate further dilation and widen the passage for the lamb to come out. She began to peel off layers of clothing as her work became more intense. Her stripped-off clothes accumulated as she threw them in a pile in the corner of the pen.

Ovenmitt decided to make his appearance then and rubbed himself along the outside edge of the pen, where The Shepherd was at work. I moved across to warm her pile of stripped clothes and told Ovenmitt to take over the coat-warming duties. At this stage, even in the bitter cold and with the wind that whistled outside the shed, The Shepherd had stripped down to a plain black T-shirt. Sweat poured from her brow as she strained to pull the lamb from the ewe. Something seemed seriously wrong. The Shepherd muttered about calling a neighbouring shepherd for help but it was now 1.30 in the morning and she thought better of it. She knew that if she really needed help, she could ask one of several local farmers or shepherds. They would drive straight here as soon as they'd pulled on their clothes, but The Shepherd hated to have to wake people up in lambing season when sleep was scarce for all.

I stretched, yawned and gave encouraging chat from my comfortable position. By this I don't mean talking like humans. That would be silly. I merely meowed at the correct time and offered general, catlike encouragement. Ovenmitt had far less sense, quite naturally, being something of an idiot at his immature inexperienced age. He jumped down into the pen repeatedly to 'help' with the strenuous business of birthing the lamb. The Shepherd was not best pleased as she was in the midst of a major struggle helping this lamb out. Ovenmitt has yet to learn that you let the human underlings do all the hard work and then take all the credit for yourself. He still tries to lend a paw during a lamb's birth.

I once saw Ovenmitt suffer something I have never experienced, a unique but harmless misfortune. Last winter, when he tried to assist The Shepherd in birthing a lamb, the ewe broke her water all over him. The Shepherd nearly collapsed laughing at him as he scarpered, soaked with birthing fluid, across the pen. He finally paused in the middle of the lambing shed to inspect the damage and commenced to lick his coat clean. A second ewe, close to lambing herself, came up to him and began to help him clean himself by licking him with great enthusiasm. What a surprised look there was on Ovenmitt's face as the ewe licked him firmly between his ears on top of his head. That sent The Shepherd into more gales of laughter. She had to grasp tightly onto the fence so that she wouldn't fall over. Our Shepherd loves to laugh and she claimed Ovenmitt gave her the best excuse of that week.

Now, though, there was no reason for laughter. 'What is wrong with this lamb?' she sighed in frustration. She had held her leg in an awkward position that kept the ewe lying down while she manipulated and pulled. Now she gave her leg a good stretch of relief.

In a normal lambing the first thing you see after the big bag of birthing fluid bursts is the lamb's two front toes emerging, as if it is diving out to begin life. Then both hooves follow, then fetlocks, then legs. The tip of the lamb's muzzle, often with its tongue sticking out, rests snugly on the fore-legs. Sometimes the lamb sticks in the birth passage if its head is too big or if the ewe hasn't fully dilated. These stuck lambs needed a mighty downward pull from The Shepherd. You will hear the ewe call out at the discomfort at the start of the pull, but when the rest of the lamb slides out with no bother, the pleased new mother gets to work immediately, enthusiastically licking clean her new lamb.

The Shepherd continued to struggle with birthing the lamb. She pulled, heaved and manipulated the lamb slowly. The ewe was now lying on her side, exhausted; The Shepherd no longer had to hold her down. The ewe panted between contractions. Despite the bitterly cold night The Shepherd dripped streams of sweat and wiped her brow on the sleeve of her T-shirt.

'I can't straighten this lamb's legs. They just won't budge. It's like they are locked in place and won't bend,' she told me. At this stage both her arms were covered in birthing goo and lubricant gel with hints of birthing blood – all of this was so far perfectly normal except for this lamb's poor jammed legs. When the birth canal fully dilated, The Shepherd reached inside the uterus and looped a strong clean string around the frozen front limbs of the lamb. She then worked the legs and head down the birthing canal, gave a massive pull and heave, and the lamb was born.

We all inspected it, closely. We knew immediately that with care it would not live long. All its limbs were bent and would not move. Its head was deformed and it was missing an eye. One rear leg was back to front.

'Oh, no, not another Schmallenberg lamb!' sighed the exhausted sweat-soaked Shepherd. A lamb that contracted this virus was an unmitigated disaster.

The exhausted ewe lay still panting from the traumatic labour but glad it was over. After a minute or two she turned her head slowly, looked back to her barely living, badly damaged lamb and muttered a motherly welcome. All evening she had looked forward to seeing her lamb, circling around, looking for it as her waters broke, but this lamb would live only three minutes before its breathing and beating heart stopped. The bitterly cold winter night would not have time to chill the life out of this newborn. If a lamb is stillborn, a ewe will clean it and paw at it to try to revive it and provoke it to stand up, but once the surrounding air has cooled the dead body, the ewe will abandon it. Many times I have seen ewes abandon lambs that are not well or emerged deformed at birth. The ewe knows instinctively that the lamb will not survive and she prefers to leave it to die quietly. If the lamb, despite its disabilities, manages to stand, the ewe will often push it away from her healthy twin lamb and not allow the disabled lamb to nurse. The ewe acts purely instinctively. She knows that she must look after the healthy lamb and in order to be efficient she must allow the other to die.

Dejected, The Shepherd rose slowly, leaned over to pick up the now-dead lamb and stepped over the pen's wooden gate. She let the ewe lie quietly to recover from her marathon struggle. I lay quite cosy, still warming her clothes. I could be sad at the death of the lamb, but it's nature's way. The cycle of birth and death continues whether I wish it to or not.

Ovenmitt jumped down as The Shepherd reached for her coat to protect herself from the chill night air. She left the shed, but soon returned with some antibiotics to protect the ewe from infection, dosed her with a vitamin mineral tonic, and brought her fresh water and hay. This ewe would not receive an orphan lamb to nurse because she had such an arduous time lambing. She would be dried off and fed low-protein food to stop her producing the milk that would have fed a normal lamb. When she recovered sufficiently, she would be sent out to live with the younger yearling ewes, called hoggets, for the rest of the winter.

Now all was done and it was after 2 a.m. The tired sad Shepherd, re-clothed in winter woollies, walked back to the farmhouse. My place on the fence was no longer warm with her clothes to sit on. I wandered back to the stable to curl up in the sweet summer-smelling hay. Ovenmitt trotted after The Shepherd, chatting away about the night's events. He hoped she would let him into the kitchen to curl up next to the warm Aga, but I knew she wouldn't allow him in. Pure wishful thinking on his part, but Ovenmitt was ever hopeful. Soon he would join me in the stable hay to curl up for a cosy night out of the bitter winter wind. Perhaps a passing mouse would provide some sport while we waited for dawn and breakfast.

The next morning, after the ewes with fresh lambs in the mothering pens had been fed, watered and checked, the lambing shed inspected and all the other sheep fed, I curled up on top of the Aga to thaw out. I listened with an ear twitch as crow calls replaced the earlier noise of sheep baaaa-ing for breakfast. Crows chattered, pecked and fought among themselves around feed troughs in the field as they found those few grains that the sheep had missed. The Shepherd sat staring at her mug of tea, eyes glazed with exhaustion. Out of my half-closed eyes I could tell it was a good clean kind of exhaustion from long hours and hard work.

13
A Mucky Month

February marks the anniversary of my arrival at Black Sheep Farm and my early days curled up in front of the Aga. In Irish lore it is also considered to be the first month of spring, although with the bitter winds, sleet and bare trees, I beg to differ.

Our best-known Irish Celtic goddess is Brigid, sacred to water, spring, fertility and healing. She is the goddess whom Irish poets adore. Brigid is celebrated in rural Ireland by many communities on the first day of February when a cross is woven from rushes, reeds or straw. This botanical cross recalls the ancient Irish pagan festival of Imbolc that marks the end of midwinter and the beginning of spring. Pagan Imbolc evolved into contemporary Candlemas and Ground-hog (Marmot) Day, which celebrate midwinter and the early hope of the coming of spring. It's thought that Saint Brigid's cross stems from pre-Christian origins and relates to the legendary symbolic Sun Cross that many think represents the four seasons.

February is also the month when we wish winter to end, but she still has some weather surprises stored for us. When Storm Darwin blasted our island on the edge of the Atlantic in February 2014, I simply curled up cosily against the Aga, not a bit worried about anything, but The Shepherd worked hard all the previous day, securing everything and anything that Darwin might blow away. She brought horses and sheep into stables and sheds. The egg-makers were locked in their house the night before. Everybody had food, water and safe shelter, since we'd had adequate warning that Storm Darwin was going to be ferocious. And so it more than proved as we had thirty trees blown down around the farm, crushing fences and sending old stone walls tumbling. Luckily, only the corner of the farmhouse was hit by a falling tree, so the damage there was just the loss of a few slates and a twisted rain gutter that we hammered back into its useful shape. The storm meant lots of repair work to fences and walls. Cutting up the fallen trees gave us firewood for years to come. The Shepherd still refers to that pile of firewood as, 'Thanks to Storm Darwin'.

However, on many days, winter still grips us in her icy fist as I make my morning rounds with The Shepherd between and over 'snow bones' scattered across the hillside's shaded runnels or rolling dips in the land. Snow bones are the white-striped remnants of snow splayed like ribs across the field. I follow The Shepherd with all our trailing canines towards this winter's feed station. We check the hay in the ring feeder to assess when a new bale needs to be brought in for resupply. As the sun fades on our still-wintry day, it seems that we will have to move a big round bale to feed sheep in the morning.

One February evening at sunset, under a rising crescent moon, a lone pen swan, as we call the females of that species, flew up our river valley. Her whiteness was painted a soft warm pink by the setting sun's last rays of light. Her wings whistled as she wound her way upriver while we watched. She called for her lost lover, but only silence greeted her. The high trill of her voice echoed across our river valley as we paused in our hillside pasture to watch her flight path above the river. The canines and I had sat to observe her airborne route from the height of our hill, so the course of her flight matched our eye-level perfectly. The Shepherd was absolutely transfixed by the beauty of this poignant tragic moment. She told us that she had heard earlier that the swan's mate, or cob, had been found killed by a fox or stray dog in a field further upriver.

As the cold air bit deeper, The Shepherd moved us back across the field towards home. When we were still some distance away from the farmhouse, all of us could detect a tantalising warm aroma of hot stew emanating from the Aga. Its scent wafted towards us through the frozen air from our kitchen chimney.

A major attribute of our Aga cooker at this time of year, besides its ability to warm and revive cold newborn lambs and take the chill off feline, canine and human bodies just in from freezing outdoors, is how its chimney draws up whatever is cooking so that those delectable scents perfume the icy outdoor air. The aroma wafts and curls its way into yards and nearby fields to wrap around anyone nearby and entice all in for our evening meal, a delicious stew of Zwartbles lamb chops. The Shepherd has insisted that I include the recipe here:

4–6 tbsp olive oil

2–3 red onions, diced

pinch sea salt

1 tbsp coarse black pepper

4 Zwartbles lamb chops (or 2lb lamb shoulder chops)

2–3 pears, peeled, cored and sliced

2–3 apples, peeled, cored and sliced

2 tbsp fresh sage (or 1 tsp rubbed sage or 2 tsp whole-leaf sage)

1 butternut squash, peeled, cored and diced

5 large carrots, peeled and sliced

Heat 2–3 tbsp. olive oil over medium heat. Add the onions, sea salt and pepper. Cook until the onions are soft, stirring often. Add 2–3 tablespoons more olive oil. Add the lamb chops and brown on each side, about 4 minutes per side. Add the pears, apples and sage. Add the squash and carrots. Cover and place in the Aga at 150°C/300°F/Gas 2 and cook for 5 hours. Remove from the oven and stir. Turn the Aga up to 180°C/350°F/Gas 4. Return the stew to the oven and cook for 45 minutes. Remove the bones before serving. Yum …

This particular evening, however, turned into something strikingly unusual. The Shepherd was greeted as we all arrived at the kitchen door by her hysterical mother. 'A bat!! A bat!! It's loose in the house. Quick, quick, catch it before it gets lost in the curtains and dies there.'

No, I hadn't a clue what was taking place, but I carried on dining from my food dish, which The Shepherd had just filled. She began to feed the Big Fellow, Bear, Pepper and the Puddlemaker.

'You can do that after you've caught the bat,' insisted The Shepherd's mother.

Thankfully, The Shepherd replied, 'Please let me feed the dogs so they're distracted before I chase a bat.'

This she did, and we all ate our fill before retiring to a cosy spot to sleep it off. That was when the ruckus started.

Miss Marley had been lazing in her large luxurious bowl on top of our tall kitchen press while Ovenmitt had been in his favourite spot curled up against the Aga to absorb all the heat he possibly could. When The Shepherd opened the door that connects our kitchen to the rest of the house's interior, the next room's lights were off, so it was pitch-dark. We heard The Shepherd telling a creature to please go towards the lights. Next thing I knew, the bat had flown into the kitchen – its arrival marked by the loud rattle from one of the big Mosse pottery bowls as Miss Marley launched herself through the air after it. Ovenmitt leapt with a thump onto the kitchen table. I galloped up the scullery steps to find Miss Marley and Ovenmitt in the midst of extraordinary aerial acrobatics trying to catch the bat. I, of course, joined in as the bat flapped, flew and circled around and around the kitchen. It darted wildly among our outstretched clawed extended paws, light bulbs hanging on electric cords from the ceiling and The Shepherd's gloved hands.

The canines simply observed the chaos, each one looking on in that bemused fashion they had perfected over time. 'Well, what do you expect me to do?'

Only the Puddlemaker, our newest canine, became excited and ran in circles. She tripped The Shepherd as she struggled to catch the spinning rotating bat while she tried to avoid treading on the Puddlemaker's rat-sized body.

At this stage of our extremely muddled and chaotic hunt, I jumped on top of a tall stool near the sink, where I acquired additional height so that when the bat dived low behind the teapots on the window sill, I could leap and easily grab it. During my carefully calculated pursuit, I perceived a very cross shout to back off and end my chase. 'Twas The Shepherd! She had miraculously caught the bat in her gloved hands. As she shouted to her mother that the bat was caught, she and I inspected it closely. It was a very common bat that we often find in our neighbourhood, called a pipistrelle.

Bats shouldn't come out of hibernation so early in such cold weather, so The Shepherd sensed something must be wrong with it. As she held it in her cupped palm with her thumb placed lightly on its body, I watched as she examined it. She noted quite quickly that it was very skinny, which is probably why it awoke too early from hibernation. It had burned up its supply of fat for the winter.

The Shepherd took one of her many one-millilitre syringes that she uses to medicate sheep whenever they might require treatment. She filled it with a mixture of water and glucose and then gently drip fed the bat by mouth. The bat lapped at each drop thirstily and drank it as soon as it appeared.

Unfortunately, there was no way to obtain mealworms for bats from a local pet shop this late in the day. So with warm water, The Shepherd mushed up some of our dried biscuit feline food. After the bat had eaten the soggy biscuit and drunk its fill, she placed it in a cardboard box covered with a cloth tea towel on a warm kitchen shelf. This bat obviously needed generous further feeding before it would be safe to return it to the stage of hibernation.

Many bats reside all over our farm. They inhabit the attic under the slate roof of our house, hollows in our trees and holes in the stone walls around our fields and garden. Whenever we repair our walls in the summer months, we often spot small holes. When we do, we place a light bit of dry moss at its front entrance overnight. Then we look the next morning to see if the moss has been pushed aside. If it has, that means a bat lives inside. We mark the hole with a red arrow since we don't wish to close the entrance to a bat's lodging.

Bats make a huge smelly mess inside the roof attic beneath the slates where they live. Their messes spatter on all the windowpanes and sills below as they fly home to roost in the gloam of dawn's half light. One evening I saw twenty bats flying inside the house. The Shepherd and her family had a house full of guests who were not in the least happy to go to bed with bats skimming above their heads in the dark and potentially tangling in their hair. This is when The Shepherd became a herder to a colony of bats. She had to move from room to room, shepherding bats out from each as quietly as possible so that our guests would not be terrified.

Bats may seem scary and ugly to you humans, but to us cats they are the most stupendous game – the chase makes me completely doolally. In fact, they are essential and useful to you because they keep the insect population down – and they're a protected species. It is illegal to use any methods to discourage their habitation. The Shepherd thinks that the best way to manage our farm's bat population is to build bat houses of a very specific design and choose special places in which to position them.

The Shepherd is not unique in her love of all creatures great and small. More and more farmers have returned to an awareness of how we need even the smallest of small micro insects, worms and fungi to be living and well fed in our soil. This helps to keep our creative food-producing practices alive and flourishing for generations to come. These minute organisms bring about a healthy bloom in our gardens and fields and reward us with a wealth of delicious food using this natural chemical enhancement, The Shepherd explained to me. By 'chemically', she means as nature had intended, not an added chemical mixture of man's prideful inventions, which are sometimes harmful to nature's natural chemistry.

The Shepherd believes that we as intelligent agrarians should respect what the American physicist Richard Feynman once said: 'Scientific knowledge is a body of statements of varying degrees of certainty – some most unsure, some nearly sure, none absolutely certain. If, in some cataclysm, all of scientific knowledge were to be destroyed, and only one sentence passed on to the next generation of creatures, what statement would contain the most information in the fewest words? I believe it is the atomic hypothesis that *all things are made of atoms – little particles that move around in perpetual motion, attracting each other when they are a little distance apart, but repelling upon being squeezed into one another.* In that one sentence, you will see, there is an enormous amount of information about the world, if just a little imagination and thinking are applied.'

The Shepherd says, 'Seeds of doubt should always be sown so thoughts can naturally grow to broaden minds and to help us to learn and experience new things every day.'

Of course, all of this fuss over bats does not deter any of us farm felines from our favourite sport whenever a bat comes inside the house. Just as I can hear the distinctive sound of an eggshell cracking from far across the fields, or Miss Marley leaps up when she hears a tin can opened, all three of us find it impossible to remain still whenever a bat flies into the house.

Often in February we'll take a walk in the wood while rain falls to see green fingers of daffodils and bluebells push up through winter-worn leaf litter. Crows will crowd crowns of winter trees. Stirred, they will lift swirling upwards like a flame of black feathers cackling in disturbed annoyance. As we walk among hazel trees with their catkins dangling, our coats will get dusted in pollen. It gets right up one's nose when licking it clean off one's fur, and sets off a few sneezes. Another storm will come howling up our valley and the winter trees will hum with the sound of its approach. Beating rain will pummel my back as I help feed meal to fields of sheep. Weather-weary, with mucky mud, thankful for my warm coat and with the knowledge that The Shepherd will soon go in for tea, I will then follow and enter the kitchen, where I'll shake off excess water and curl up next to the Aga.

Afterword

There is a lovely natural silence as I sit high on a grassy hill. I hear no tractor, car or human voice; no sound vibrates in my furry ear. Yes, trees rustle, birds sing, a grey squirrel scolds, crows call, a distant hawk screams, a buzzard mews, a cow bellows, but the ground beneath me breathes in the thawing warmth of a southern breeze. As I sit still in silence, my busy mind works. I can hear the soil inhale. Drip by drip, it pops, sucks and squelches as ice crystals melt and moisture soaks back into the soil.

As frost melts, rich earth wafts a fresh perfume of grass, leaves and weeds. Mellowed manure, decomposed and digested by worms and the network of fungi and moulds, belches bacteria back into the warming air with help from the morning breeze. In much of the land on our planet Earth, the richness of our six inches of fertile soil are what feed us, what we are made of, where we came from and where we will return.

As The Shepherd says, 'Blessed are those who recognise, feed, mind, tend and understand the soil for the benefit of others. Those who abuse soil, use it, plunder it, poison it and worship many materials drawn or mined from deep beneath – they still have to eat.'

The Shepherd tells me she senses a shift in the world, a hunger from those whose lives are surrounded by concrete to return to the soil and to respect it, even venerate it, and esteem those who care for and live by it. The cultural transition of respect for those who work the land to provide food began to change long ago when small communities traded food as a commodity for material things. Before oil became the substance by which the human world is fuelled, clothed, fertilised and heated, the soil's enriched health was able to feed, clothe and heat everyone.

She is right, I suppose. In my years roaming the fields of Black Sheep Farm, I have learned how important our soil is, and how good it feels beneath my spread paws. Well-tended and looked-after earth is good for you and to you. When next you sit down to a meal, thank the earth and whatever God you praise for your existence. Healthy soil permits you to survive on our beautiful blue planetary marble that floats through our space in the universe.

I am forever grateful that The Shepherd took up Jaszia's

suggestion to go and look at a cat in the exotic novelty toilet-seat shop all those many years ago and brought me to Black Sheep Farm. I have enjoyed learning the conversion from urban ignorance to rural knowledge. I think it's fair to say nothing compares to the adventures I've experienced and the work that I've endured while living on Black Sheep Farm.

Acknowledgements

I must thank Bodacious firstly for allowing me to write what I think I know about his farm life story. He has very strong opinions and I had to follow his strict instructions. He has been interviewed many times but never written a book before.

As we enter into the final edits of this creation for Bodacious I would love to thank all those who were so very kind to help me with all sorts of things. There are many but I must limit myself to a few important people, like Pat, Alex and Sally who were there whenever I called for their help. Thank you to my agent Marianne Gunn O'Connor who fell in love with Bodacious's story and believed in my ability to tell it. Charlie Redmayne the CEO of Harper Collins who loved the pitch and took a chance on an Irish blanket designing shepherd who had a cat that could spin a biographical tail. Vicky Eribo my Harper Collins editor who spent several days and many hours going over editorial corrections with me on the phone after the Beast from the East clashed with Storm Emma to produce a blizzard of epic proportions and a time delaying factor that no farmer could compete with. The design team that produced such a zinging book cover from some of my farm life photographs. Everyone at HarperCollins and last but not least the Harper Collins publicity team.

Alison Walsh was a wonderful guiding hand that I could cling onto as I dived into the unknown having never written a book before. Alison edited and instructed with such kind attention and asked excellent questions which I found I could easily respond to. My wonderful parents Julia and Richard Crampton helped me in innumerable ways that are beyond counting. In particular they were great at keeping me in line and facts correct about family history. I also learned loads from my father due to his editing ability and knowledge. I am grateful to nighttime lambing observer Susan Wilde who came to stay for twelve days. She inspected the sheep shed nightly looking for and waiting for sheep to lamb. She only called me when she felt something was amiss or that a ewe was indeed lambing. This enabled me to have a relatively full night's sleep of five to six hours unless Susan called. There was one memorable twenty-four hours in which I had little sleep, loads of lambing and I even managed to get some writing done between meals and husbandry.

The veterinarian Tommy Heffernan read through my manuscript to make sure I made no huge husbandry or veterinarian mistakes. I'm sure there are those in the farming world who have different technics to accomplish similar husbandry endeavors. Deborah Robson kindly dealt with my wool questions with wonderful detailed emails and her fantastic source book 'The Fleece and Fiber Sourcebook'. If there are any mistakes, they are mine alone in not understanding correctly what I have been told by the expert opinion of this well informed individual.

Another indispensable kind neighbor was Simon Mosse for responding without question whenever a farming issue occurred in which I needed his wonderful tractor or shepherding knowledge. I hope that now this book is written and if enough people buy and enjoy it Bodacious might be able to buy me a tractor on his earnings.

There is a plethora of others I could mention but that would be a book unto itself. Just know that it took a community of encouragement, support and help to enable me to write this my first book while also farming.